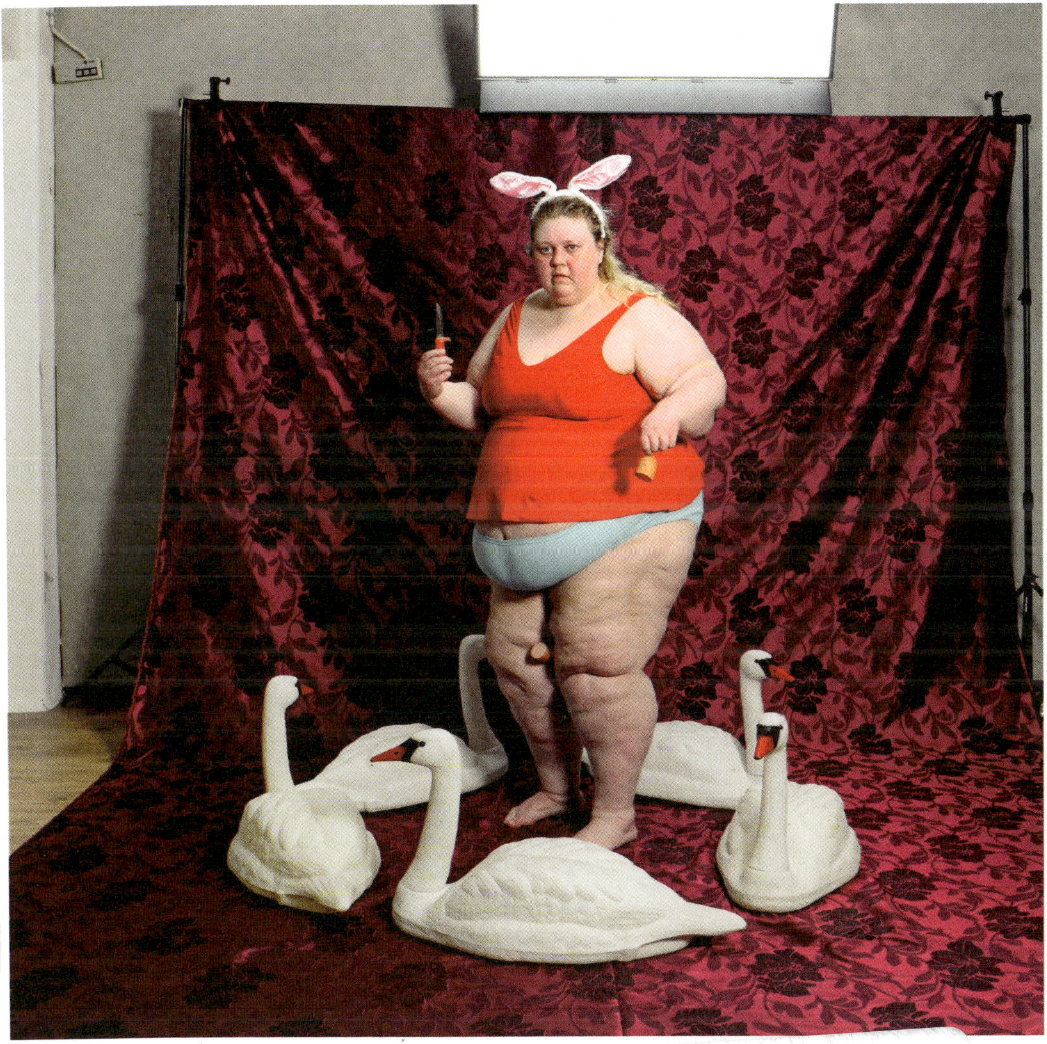

1

IIU SUSIRAJA

A STYLE CALLED A DEAD FISH

Iiu Susiraja makes photographs that echo in the mind: once you see them, they're hard to forget. And yet, she has had few occasions to share her works in the United States. It is therefore an honor to present her first museum exhibition in the US at MoMA PS1, bringing her singular practice to wider audiences. Carefully crafted but distinctly unfettered by propriety, Susiraja's photographs resonate with contemporary queries around the politics of self-imaging.

PS1 has a long history of showing international artists at critical points in their careers, and this exhibition comes at an opportune moment, highlighting fifteen years of Susiraja's practice—from her first photographs to new work made just months before the exhibition's opening. I thank Jody Graf, Assistant Curator at PS1, for bringing Susiraja's work into our orbit through both the exhibition and this book. Together, the curator and I would also like to thank the lenders to the exhibition as well as Makasiini Contemporary and Nino Mier Gallery. Mike Egan, an early supporter of Susiraja's work, was a key interlocutor. We are also thankful to Julia Schäfer for the beautiful design of this catalogue, our Program Production team for their steadfast efforts to make the presentation a reality, and the entire staff at PS1 for the creativity and enthusiasm they bring to all of our endeavors.

I am incredibly grateful to the entire Board of MoMA PS1, led by the inimitable Sarah Arison, for their unwavering support of our efforts to highlight experimental practices at PS1. Similarly, we thank our municipal partners: Laurie Cumbo and the New York City Department of Cultural Affairs; Donovan Richards, Queens Borough President; Julie Won, Council Member; and the New York City

Council. I thank Glenn D. Lowry, The David Rockefeller Director of The Museum of Modern Art, for his continuous support.

This exhibition would not have been possible without the support of Frame Contemporary Art Finland, the Consulate General of Finland in New York, and the Finnish Cultural Institute in New York. Our gratitude goes out to Makasiini Contemporary and Nino Mier Gallery for their assistance with this catalogue, which will surely serve as a great resource for the future.

Finally, we thank Iiu Susiraja for sharing her world with us, and allowing us to share it in turn.

Ruba Katrib
Curator & Director of Curatorial Affairs, MoMA PS1

Any time you slice a salami, you take a risk.
—Andy Warhol

Iiu Susiraja has lived nearly her entire life in Turku,
Finland, on the lip of the Baltic Sea. She began taking
photographs in 2007, at the age of thirty-two, and
soon turned the camera on herself. From the beginning,
Susiraja has depicted herself within interior settings—
almost always her own home or that of her parents—as
she interacts with precisely chosen objects of varying
degrees of banality and drollness. Rubber duckies,
freshly pressed shirts, balloons, smoked fish, hot dogs,
umbrellas, and teddy bears—to name just a few—find
themselves suspended from, balanced on, or held by her
body. Sometimes, not always, she appears in states of
undress, exposing her bare flesh. Intimate yet decidedly
unsentimental, her works are both achingly spare and
abundant with understated theater.

Woman (2010), an early self-portrait, exemplifies the
tempered, ludic drama of Susiraja's practice [fig. 1].
Wearing a dark dress and a white knit cap, she faces the
camera, serene and composed, her gaze tilted slyly—a
touch religiously—upward. You might almost miss the
two small fish tucked into the bands of her gloved hands.
Such whispers of absurdity are key to Susiraja's practice,
which is often discussed in terms of its "edginess"
and "humor." These affects are certainly at play, but,
like *Woman*, many of Susiraja's works foster a quiet,
contemplative kind of looking and draw from orthodox
compositional tropes like the still life, *vanitas*, and self-

portraiture. Her photographs may be funny, but they are never a joke. Their deadpan quality emerges in tandem with an unnerving elegance that recalls the exacting attention to material particularities displayed in Northern Renaissance paintings—Rogier van der Weyden's *Portrait of a Lady* (ca. 1460), for example, comes to mind [fig. 2]. Geographical distance and more than five hundred years separate these portraits, but they share what art historian Svetlana Alpers calls a "descriptive" impulse that, as distinguished from the narrative temperament of the Italian Renaissance, relishes detail and carefully charts the act of looking itself.[1] Susiraja focuses attention on the material coordinates of her world as they existed for the camera in that singular moment—not what happened before or after. The *what* overshadows the *why*, transforming the question into a *why not* and thereby placing pressure on a societal need to justify, explain, and make sense of every action that troubles the norm. Her works occupy space without apology.

Susiraja was trained as a textile designer before turning to photography, and her early works brim with fabric: scraps of embroidery, lace tablecloths, sweatshirts, and checkered curtains encroach on center stage. In the first self-portraits she took, from 2007, her head is sheathed, almost punitively, in sack-like cloths that obscure her features [fig. 3]. *Large-scale cleaning* (2008) depicts a nubby, striped runner rug cascading vertically over her body, and *When I touch the flowers* (2010)— one of her few bona fide still-lifes—features a carnation drooping under the weight of crisp white cotton. This attention to cloth and clothing continues throughout her entire practice, but the role of fabric shifts from masking or shrouding skin to accompanying and extending it. Her face appears, and then her body; she begins to lock eyes with the camera, her gaze flickering between impassive, mischievous, and plaintive. It is difficult to think of another look simultaneously so laden and so vacant. That of Iris, the protagonist of Finnish director Aki Kaurismäki's 1990 film *The Match Factory Girl*, who stares blankly in painful satisfaction as she waits for those who have harmed her to drink libations laced with rat poison, might come closest.

It is tempting to read a progression of increasing confidence in Susiraja's work, a shedding of shyness that fits neatly into filmic narratives of overcoming obstacles or finding one's "inner" self, however twisted the path. Susiraja's more recent works show her naked flesh, which, because she is fat—a term I use here purposefully and with respect, as opposed to pathologizing words such as "obese" or "overweight"[2]— has been interpreted as a statement of bravery and "body positivity" on the basis that she must be seeking to cast herself as beautiful or shift societal standards of what counts as such.[3] Without discounting the liberating effect her photographs might have, Susiraja has demurred from such interpretations, stating, "It's funny that people think that my purpose is to criticize beauty ideals or social issues. I have no such intentions. These things come afterwards. My starting point is purely the object and how it relates to me."[4] "The object," she goes on, "is a tool for experiencing partnerships."[5] Through her pas de deux with objects, Susiraja suggests the sheer materiality of the self as one substance within a continuum of all the myriad things we rub up against, put on, take off, hold, repel, and ingest. An extended dance between concealment and exposure, self and other, pervades, raising questions about what we are comfortable baring and where the subcutaneous— the fantasy of a true interior—begins. Perhaps it is not so much beauty that is in question as *desire*—something arguably slipperier and held closer to the chest.

Susiraja starts her work by making lists: "I don't actually do much consciously at all, other than list objects on paper and go and fetch them," she has stated.[6] *Good Behavior*, an early series begun in 2008, crystallized this approach to incorporating objects as both props and collaborators in scenarios that, as the title ironically suggests, involve behaviors that test the limits of propriety. Things are not where they are supposed to be but exactly where she wants them—a simple yet loaded provocation made all the more so because, as Susiraja has noted, "if a fat person behaves badly ... then they are doubly misbehaving. Being fat is a transgression in itself."[7] In *Broom* (2010), she poses in her kitchen with a broom suspended horizontally under the folds of her breasts. In another work from this series, *Training* (2010), she stands on a treadmill with two braided loaves of bread dangling, like bloated earrings, from either side of her head. *Spruce* (2010) captures her next to a Christmas tree. A lone string of lights hangs on the tree, while Susiraja is more adorned: she sports a brightly colored dress, a birdhouse on her head, and a ping-pong ball stuffed in her mouth, casting her own body as armature for ornamentation. Christmas trees, for many, symbolize something *special*, or perhaps the desire for specialness—for something to disrupt the monotony of the days. Susiraja's work plays with this idea of specialness, how we accord it (*have you been good?*) and how, with a slight shift in placement or perspective, something can turn from magic to mundane and back.

Much like a spruce that is decorated, cherished, and then tossed to the curb, Susiraja's process involves staging and striking scenes, recalling Roland Barthes's observation that "it is not ... by Painting that Photography touches art, but by Theater."[8] She carefully conceives and sets up each composition, then photographs it using a self-timer.[9] In this, they evoke

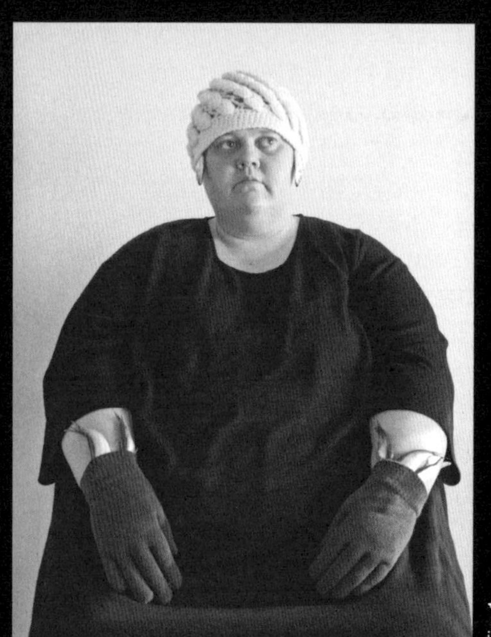

Fig. 1
Iiu Susiraja
Woman, 2010
Chromogenic print
33 ½ x 25 ⅛" (85.1 x 63.8 cm)

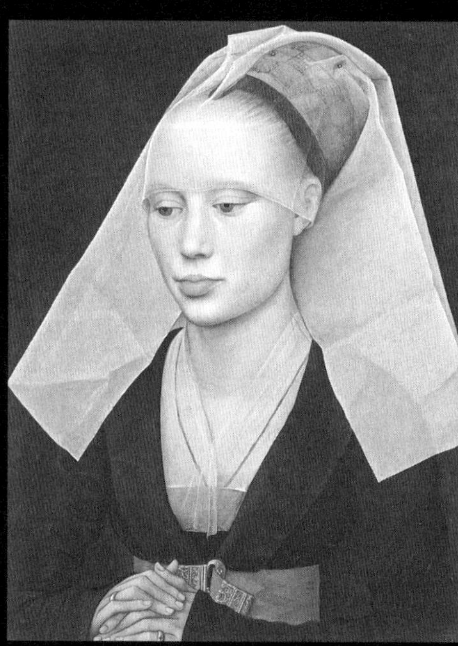

Fig. 2
Rogier van der Weyden
Portrait of a Lady, c. 1460
Oil on panel
24 x 21 x 4 ½" (60.9 x 53.3 x 11.4 cm) (framed)
Andrew W. Mellon Collection, National Gallery of Art,
Washington, DC

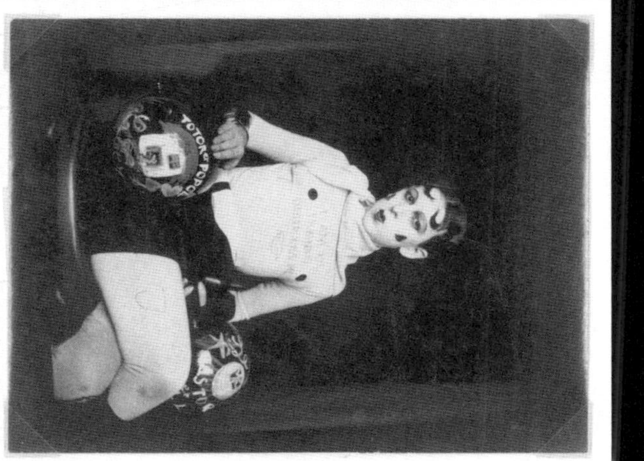

Fig. 4
Claude Cahun
I am in training don't kiss me, 1927
Photograph
15 3/4 x 10 4/5 x" (53 x 40 cm)
Jersey Heritage Museum

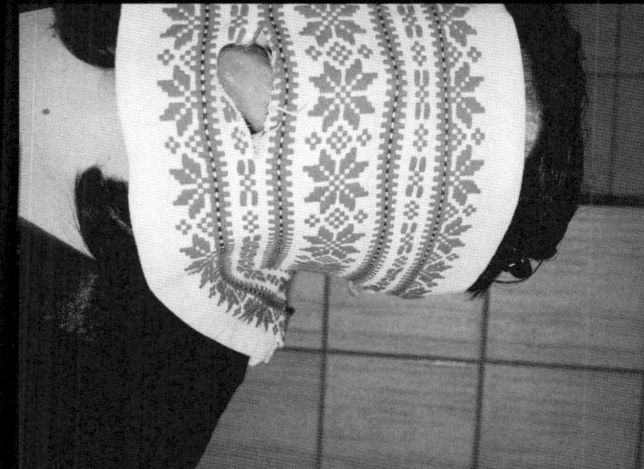

Fig. 3
Iiu Susiraja
Thick emotions, 2007
Chromogenic print
Dimensions variable

precedents in a legacy of staged photography, such as Claude Cahun, Cindy Sherman, Catherine Opie, and Patty Chang, each of whom poses for the lens in states of both vulnerability and disguise [fig. 4]. Susiraja points to Finnish artist Heli Rekula's *Hyperventilation* (1993) as a touchstone influence. The striking image of Rekula squatting, wearing a gas mask attached to tubes inserted into her vagina and anus, resonates with Susiraja's own approach to perceived discomfort (on the part of both artist and viewer) and caustic pleasure.[10] Performance, even if decidedly private in the moment of its execution, resides at the core of Susiraja's practice, as the many videos she has made in concert with her photographs also make clear. Each about one minute long and shot in a single take, the videos capture Susiraja in flagrante: spitting into an umbrella and turning it overhead (*Raining 1*, 2017), for example, or removing a vase from a glass cabinet, licking it from top to bottom, and setting it carefully back (*Vitrin*, 2017) [fig. 5].

The performative aspect of Susiraja's work is undeniable, but it raises the question of what, exactly, she is playing at. She characteristically complicates the matter, stating: "I don't try to take any role, I want to be as real as possible. As blank as possible. For me, being blank is the same as being real."[11] This "blankness," felt so keenly in her poker face, can at times heighten the drama, but it also cuts through the artifice of theater. Performing suggests a more or less intentional act for some kind of audience, but *to perform* can also mean to get something done, like performing a task or "fetching an object," as Susiraja has described her practice. Far from the narrative structure of a script, her scenarios obliquely take up the logic of the to-do list or instruction manual: they set up a goal and achieve it. Her work puts a new gloss on the kind of task-based performance that emerged in the 1960s and 1970s—Richard Serra's iconic *Verb List* (1967) taken to a slapstick extreme. In Susiraja's case, she is both subject and object of the verb, treating her own body as one material among many "to splash/to knot/to spill/ to droop."

Susiraja takes all of her photographs indoors, and almost exclusively within her own home—a site that is convenient, isolated, and psychologically charged, as well as the traditional realm of a particular kind of task-based labor.[12] Domestic objects and household tools proliferate in her photos, from the early *Broom* (2010) through *Duster* (2019), in which she strikes a classic pin-up pose—legs open, arms behind her head— with a duster protruding from her navel and a yellow rubber glove drooping from beneath each breast. In *Iloinen morsian (Happy bride)* (2017), she perches on the edge of a faux-baroque bed; her face is veiled with lace, through which she grips a large sausage in her mouth. A purposely ham-fisted and sexualized questioning of gendered roles and chores shines through in such pieces, reminiscent of Martha Rosler's exaggerated mishandling of cooking tools in *Semiotics of the Kitchen* (1975) [fig. 6]. This critique resides more implicitly within most of Susiraja's work. A 2022 exhibition at Nino Mier Gallery in Los Angeles, for example, featured a suite of photographs in which she lounges half-naked on her bed with an assortment of playful items, such as an umbrella full of rubber duckies (*Fountain*, 2021) [fig. 7], Santa heads (*Blue Lagoon*, 2021), or a pile of sliced bread and a jar of Nutella covering her crotch (*Good Morning*, 2021). It comes as a (fitting) surprise to learn that the series is titled, flatly, *Women's Work*.

As in the *Women's Work* photos, Susiraja often depicts herself torpid—lying down, sitting, or standing very still. At times she seems to dissolve into the interior

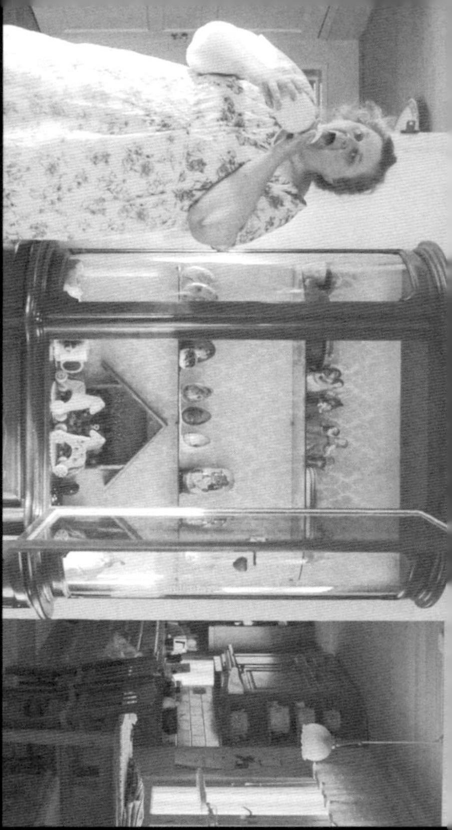

Fig. 5
Iiu Susiraja
Still from *Vitrin*, 2017
Video (color, sound)
1 min, 4 sec

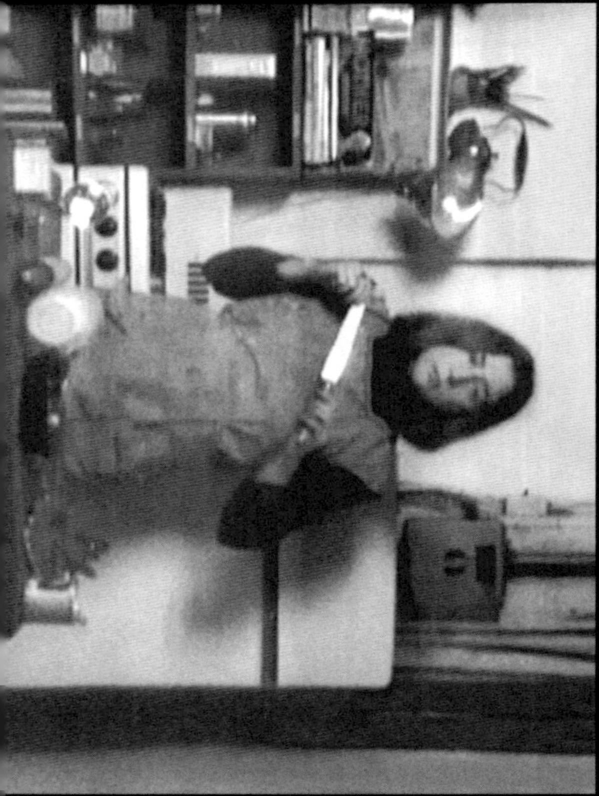

Fig. 6
Martha Rosler
Still from *Semiotics of the Kitchen*, 1975
Video (b/w, sound)
6 min, 9 sec
Courtesy Martha Rosler and Electronic Arts Intermix (EAI), New York

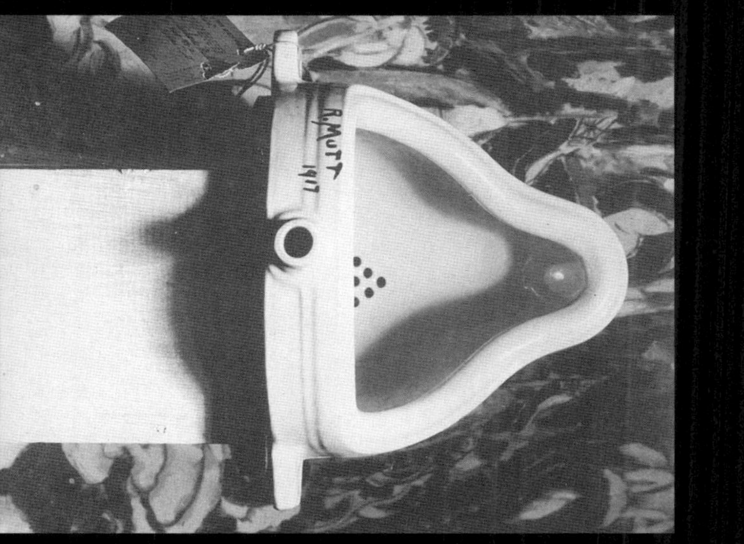

Fig. 8
Marcel Duchamp
Fountain, 1917
Photograph by Alfred Stieglitz, 1917
Gelatin silver print

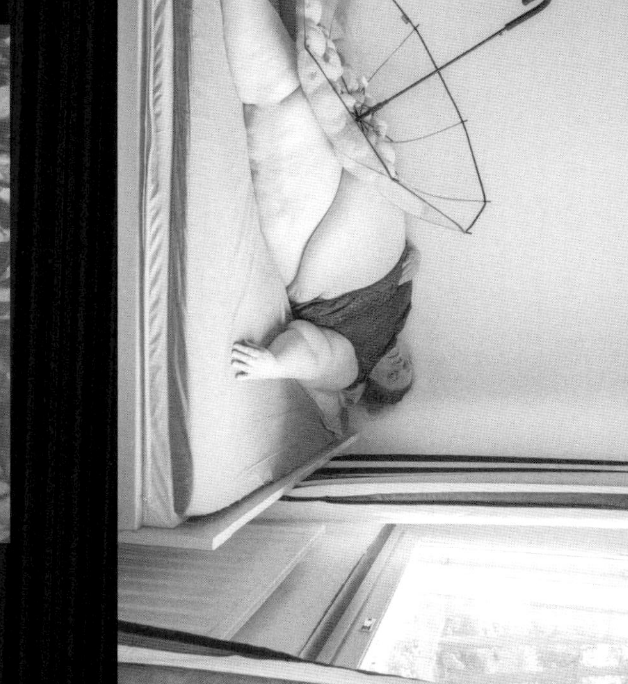

Fig. 7
Iiu Susiraja
Fountain, 2021
Chromogenic print
26 x 38" (66 x 96.5 cm)

that surrounds her or to turn into an object herself.
As Johanna Fateman puts it, Susiraja presents as a
"deadpan protagonist—or a jarring centerpiece," an
ambiguity that challenges the distinctions between
subject and object.[13] Some works seem to ape classic
odalisque imagery of women lounging elegantly,
as in the series *Afternoon on the divan* (2016) or the
photograph *Patongit (French loafs)* (2017), in which
she sinks into a sofa with two baguettes protruding
from between her legs in the shape of a cross. Western
society demands women be both sexually passive
and domestically productive; Susiraja confuses these
roles, twisting her passivity into something darker (*A
style called a dead fish*, as she titled a 2018 photograph)
and turning ostensibly productive tools into docile
and flaccid props. Workout equipment appears often,
but neutered—as in *Airplane* (2020), for which she
poses on an elliptical machine, stationary and holding
plastic bags of air in her outstretched hands, or *Ankle
weights* (2017), in which strings of hot dogs wrap around
each ankle. This swapping of heaviness and levity is
characteristic of her practice and points, satirically, at the
burden of navigating the world with the weight of untold
symbolic phalluses dragging you down.

Though more than a century has passed since Marcel
Duchamp designated a urinal a sculpture (*Fountain*,
1917) [fig. 8] and Elsa von Freytag-Loringhoven mounted
a lead plumbing pipe on a piece of wood and called
it *God* (ca. 1917), contemporary art is often dogged by
suspicions that an insufficient amount of effort has gone
into its creation, a suspicion with which Susiraja seems
to purposefully toy. In a 2014 interview with *Dazed*
magazine, she recounts, somewhat tickled, an email she
received from an unknown sender that read: "Go and
get a proper job."[14] The pleasure she takes in subverting
the presumed primacy of work over leisure also

confuses any simple triangulation between "art-work," "work-work," and fun. It calls to mind a retort Andy Warhol once gave to a question about the "riskiness" of being an artist: "What do you mean, an 'artist'? An artist can slice a salami, too! Why do people think artists are special? It's just another job." Warhol's point is not that there is no risk, but rather that you take a risk "any time you slice a salami."[15] In other words, all work can be special, and creating specialness is work. Susiraja's "slicing" (both metaphorical and not) pokes at suspicions of "lazy" art while alluding to a larger Western discomfort with perceived excess, pleasure, gluttony, and sloth—a discomfort mapped more reproachfully onto fat bodies. She sets askew prohibitions against purposelessness that caution us to "eat food, not play with it," "rest for sleep, not leisure," and "have sex for reproduction, not pleasure." In doing so, she asks viewers to consider who is entitled to enjoy such "sinful" luxuries or hold appetites so unbridled.

In the book *Cruel Optimism*, theorist Laurent Berlant touches on the doubled-edged roles that appetite and desire play in sustaining dreams of a "good life" during historical moments in which the payoff for proper behavior is not guaranteed and society no longer underwrites the "organizational fantasies" we are taught to harbor. Even as these dreams become increasingly necessary "ballast[s] against wearing out," desire can often, they argue, also contribute to our own attrition.[16] "A relation of cruel optimism exists," they write, "when something you desire is actually an obstacle to your flourishing. It might involve food, or a kind of love; it might be a fantasy of the good life, or a political project."[17] Eating, as both a necessity for life and, for Berlant, a pleasure that can harm when overindulged, exemplifies such cruel optimism for the theorist. It can also place the self in suspension even as it buttresses it: "Like other small pleasures, it can produce an experience of self-abeyance, of floating sideways."[18]

In Susiraja's hands, desires, appetites, and wants—those optimistic impulses manifested through proximity and ingestion—find themselves decoupled from narratives of betterment and satisfaction, escaping the tacit moralizing around "obesity" that Berlant's argument harbors.[19] Susiraja releases the pressure valve on optimization, defanging cruelty and guilt. The ice cream cone ends up on her face instead of in her mouth; the stilettos are taped to her calves rather than placed on her feet. This is the "good life genre" gone wrong, a kind of happy pessimism, so to speak, in which desire itself is made to float sideways. Abjection—a word at times used to describe the incorporation of bodily fluids and food in Susiraja's work—has often been theorized as troubling the line between self and other through the impulse to ingest what is outside the self, to turn the inside out. "There is nothing like the abjection of self to show," Julia Kristeva writes, "that all abjection is in fact recognition of the *want* on which any being, language, or desire is founded."[20] Susiraja's works touch on this foundational and meddlesome want. There are so many ways for things to get close, she seems to suggest, but you can never really keep them. In a photograph taken in December 2022 but titled *Happy Valentines Day (Big Heart)*, she sits on a stool in her kitchen, her naked body covered by a heart-shaped helium balloon that she holds close to the chest, like armor. It appears simultaneously bulky, burdensome, and exquisite. "Today I just took the air out of the Valentine's Day balloons," she writes to me a week later. I imagine the pleasure of watching that big, shiny heart deflate.

1   Svetlana Alpers, *The Art of Describing: Dutch Art in the Seventeenth Century* (Chicago: University of Chicago Press, 1983).

2   For a discussion of pathologizing terminology, see Marilyn Wann, "Fat Studies: An Invitation to Revolution," in *The Fat Studies Reader*, ed. Esther Rothblum and Sondra Solovay (New York: New York University Press, 2009), xii.

3   Susiraja has stated, for example, "Many people think that I'm really brave, but I actually think that it would be much braver to take pictures of other people, to be a news photographer or to go into strangers' houses." Quoted in Paula Korte, "'I Can Do Whatever I Like to Myself': An Interview with Iiu Susiraja," in *Iiu Susiraja: Dry Joy*, ed. Kati Kivinen (Helsinki: Museum of Contemporary Art Helsinki, 2019), 59.

4   Korte, "'I Can Do Whatever I Like to Myself,'" 61.

5   Korte, "'I Can Do Whatever I Like to Myself,'" 52.

6   Korte, "'I Can Do Whatever I Like to Myself,'" 62.

7   Korte, "'I Can Do Whatever I Like to Myself,'" 63. Susiraja notes the influence of media theorist Kathleen K. Rowe on this thinking.

8   Roland Barthes, *Camera Lucida: Reflections on Photography* (New York: Hill & Wang, 1982), 31.

9   Her images are almost always illuminated with daylight, though she has recently begun to use flash as well.

10 Iiu Susiraja, email to the author, December 13, 2022.

11 Korte, "'I Can Do Whatever I Like to Myself,'" 60.

12 Early on, Susiraja took many photos in her parents' house. She has on rare occasions taken photos elsewhere, including a hotel room in New York (see *Badminton*, p. 106, and *Pinnochio*, p. 108), and, for a brief stint, she used a studio in Turku (see *Sausage cupid*, 2019, p. 115).

13 Johanna Fateman, "Iiu Susiraja's Portraits Are More Than a Dare," *The New Yorker*, May, 22, 2022, www.newyorker.com/culture/photo-booth/iiu-susirajas-self-portraits-are-more-than-a-dare.

14 Ben Jolley, "Iiu Susiraja's body talking selfies," *Dazed*, October 15, 2014, www.dazeddigital.com/artsandculture/article/22129/1/iiu-susirajas-body-talking-selfies.

15 Andy Warhol, *The Philosophy of Andy Warhol: From A to B and Back Again* (New York: Harcourt Brace Jovanovich, 1975), 178.

16 Lauren Berlant, "Slow Death (Sovereignty, Obesity, Lateral Agency)," *Critical Inquiry* 33, no. 4 (Summer 2007): 778.

17 Lauren Berlant, *Cruel Optimism* (Durham, NC: Duke University Press, 2011), 1.

18 Berlant, "Slow Death," 778.

19 For a critical discussion of Berlant's moralizing, see Amalle Dublon, "Mariah Carey Remix, 25th Anniversary Edition (feat. Theodor Adorno and Lauren Berlant)," *Art in America*, November 9, 2022, www.artnews.com/art-in-america/columns/mariah-carey-philosophy-honey-1234646032/.

20 Julia Kristeva, *Powers of Horror: An Essay on Abjection*, trans. Leon S. Roudiez (New York: Columbia University Press, 1982), 145.

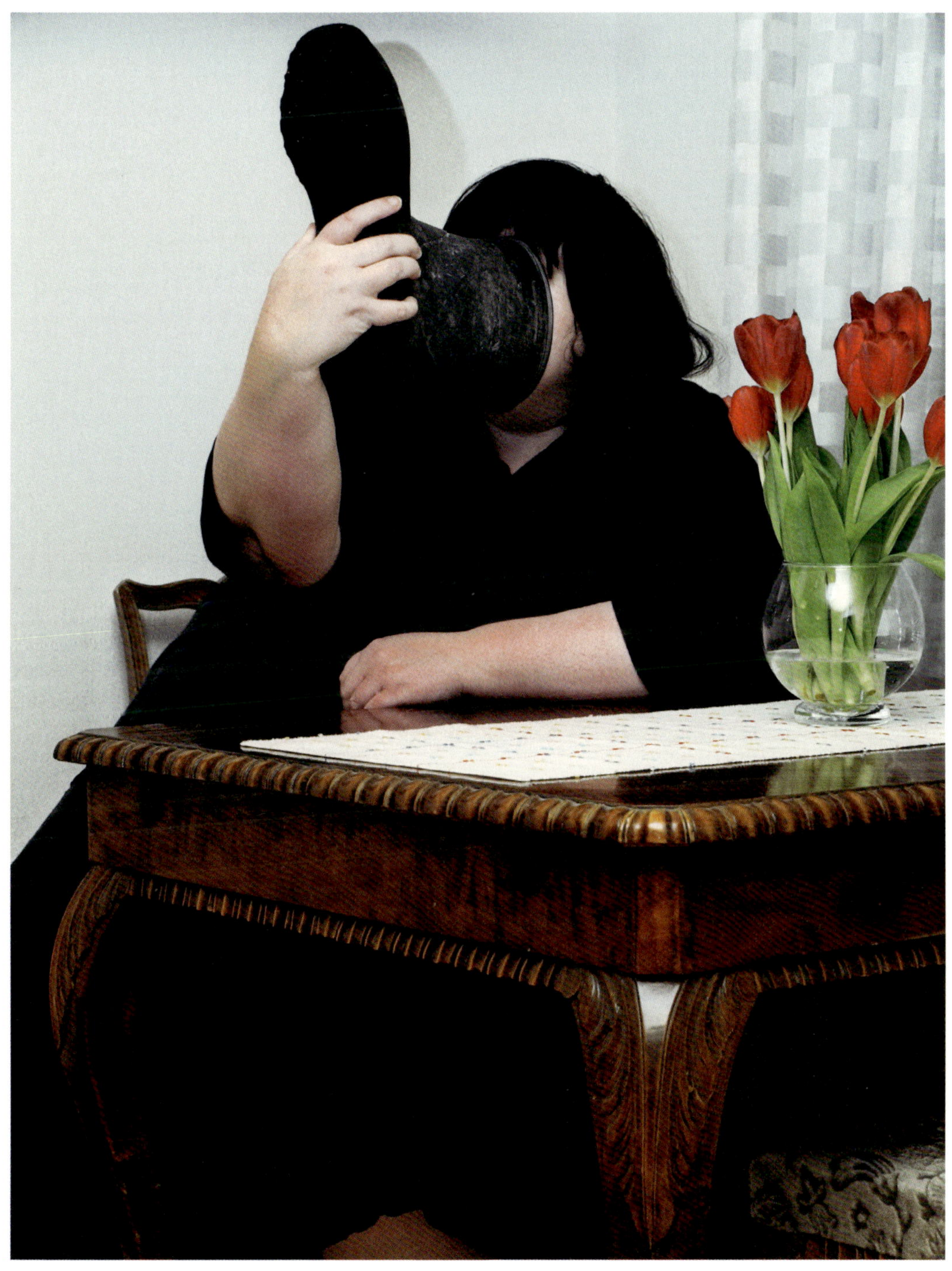

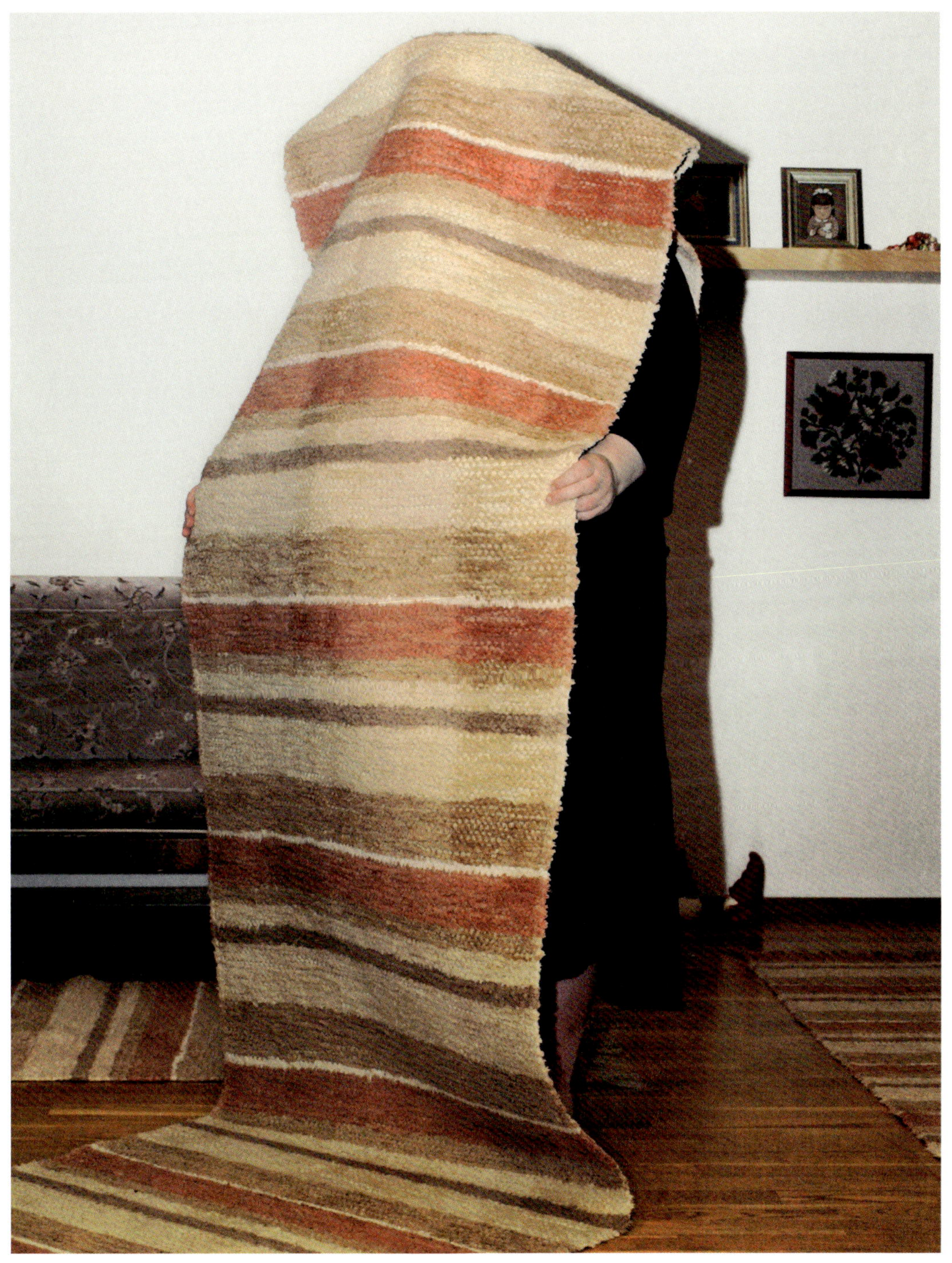

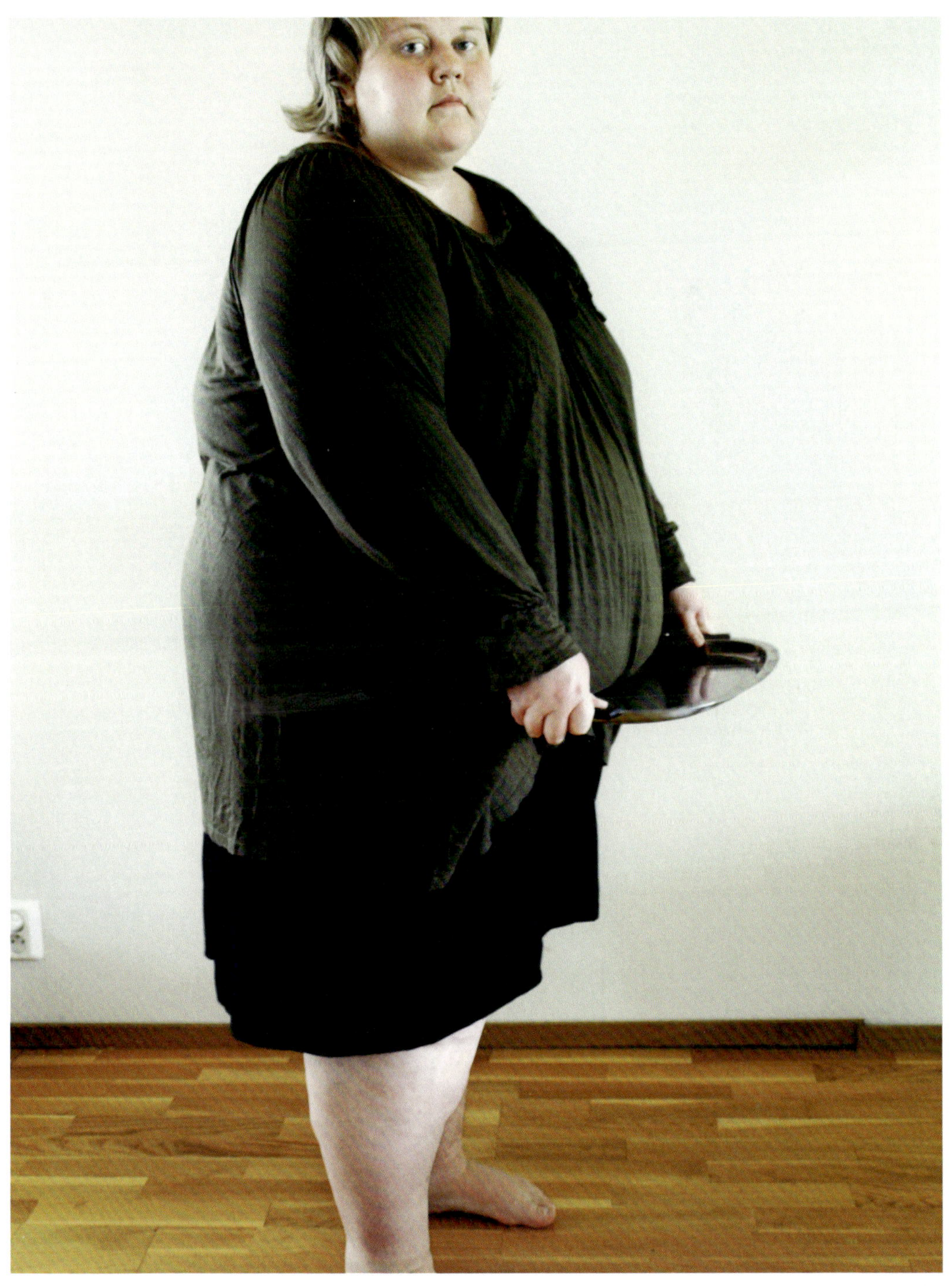

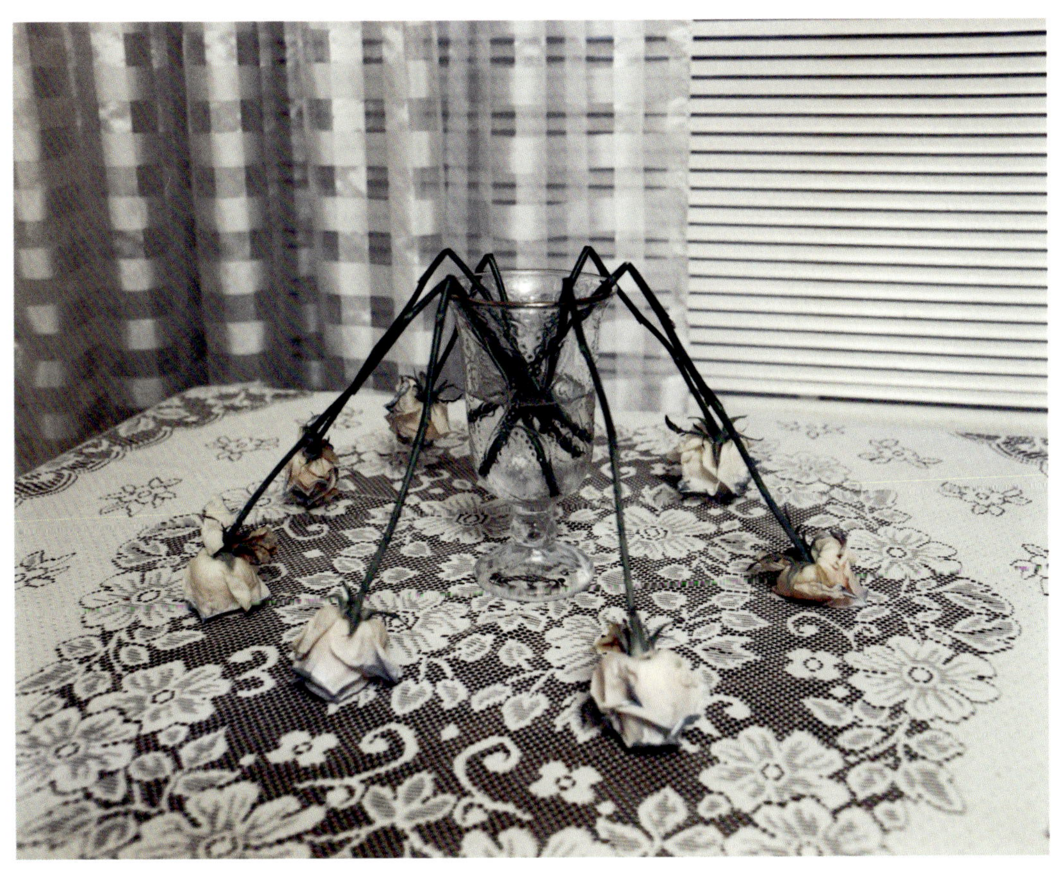

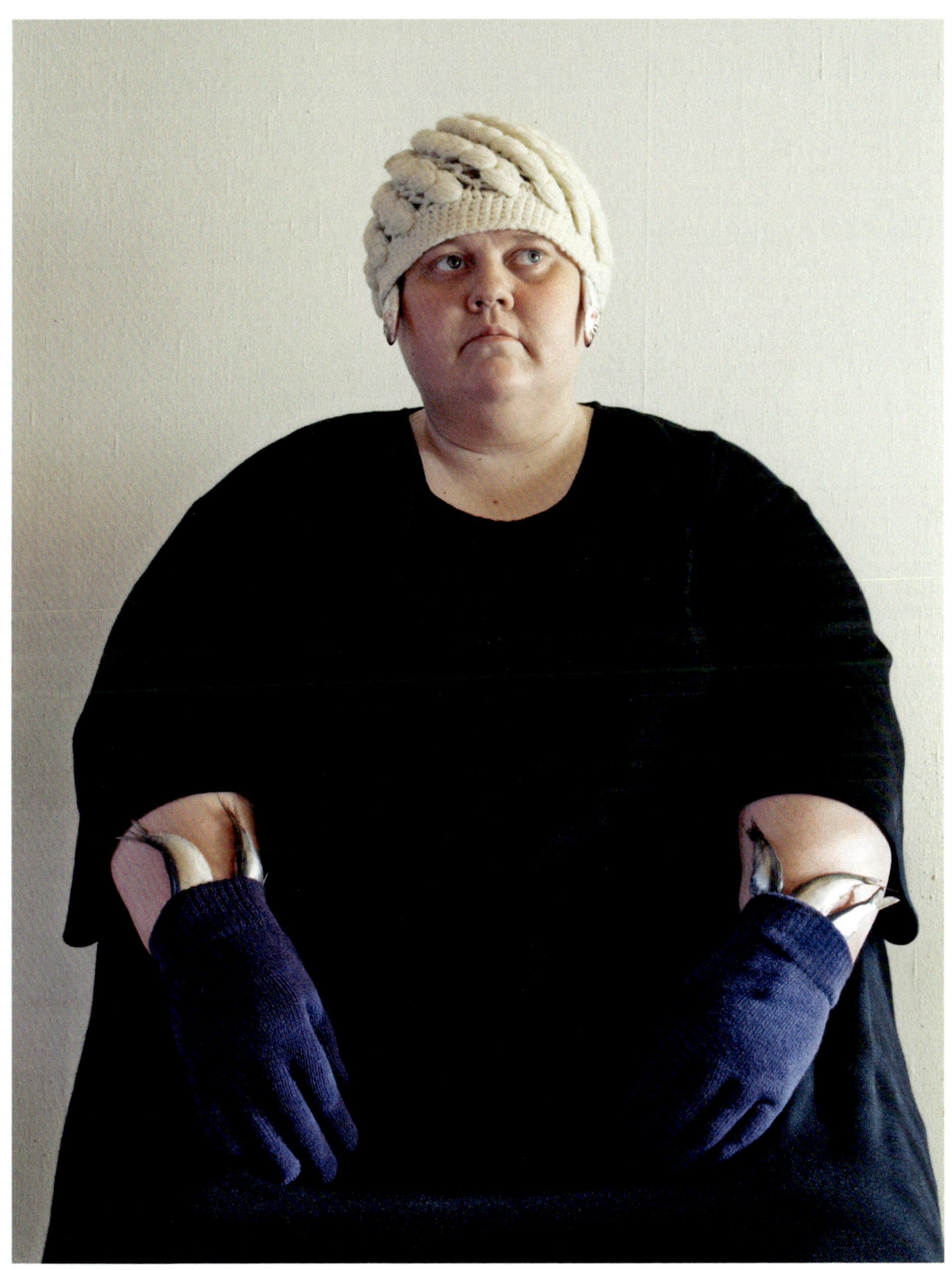

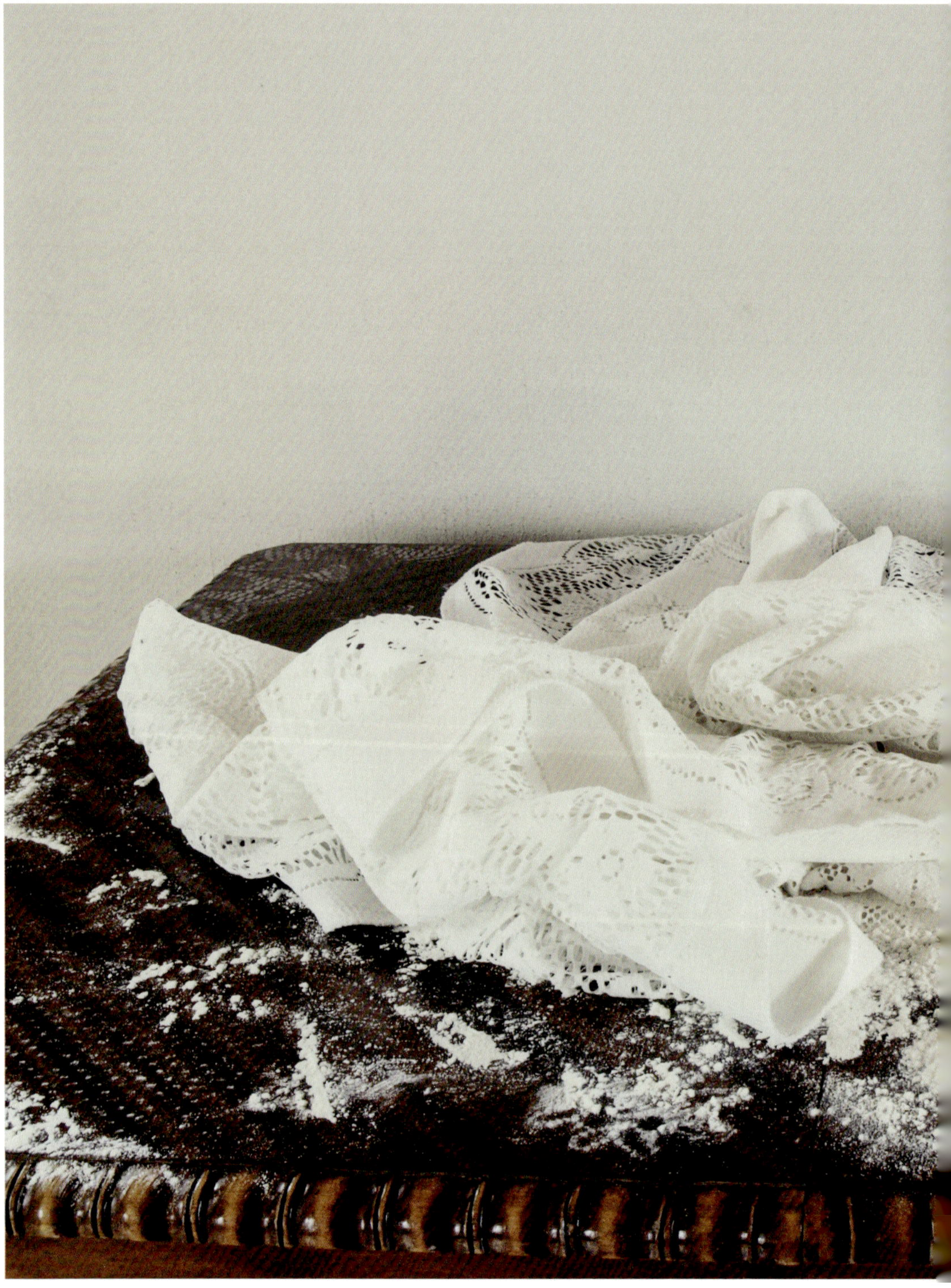

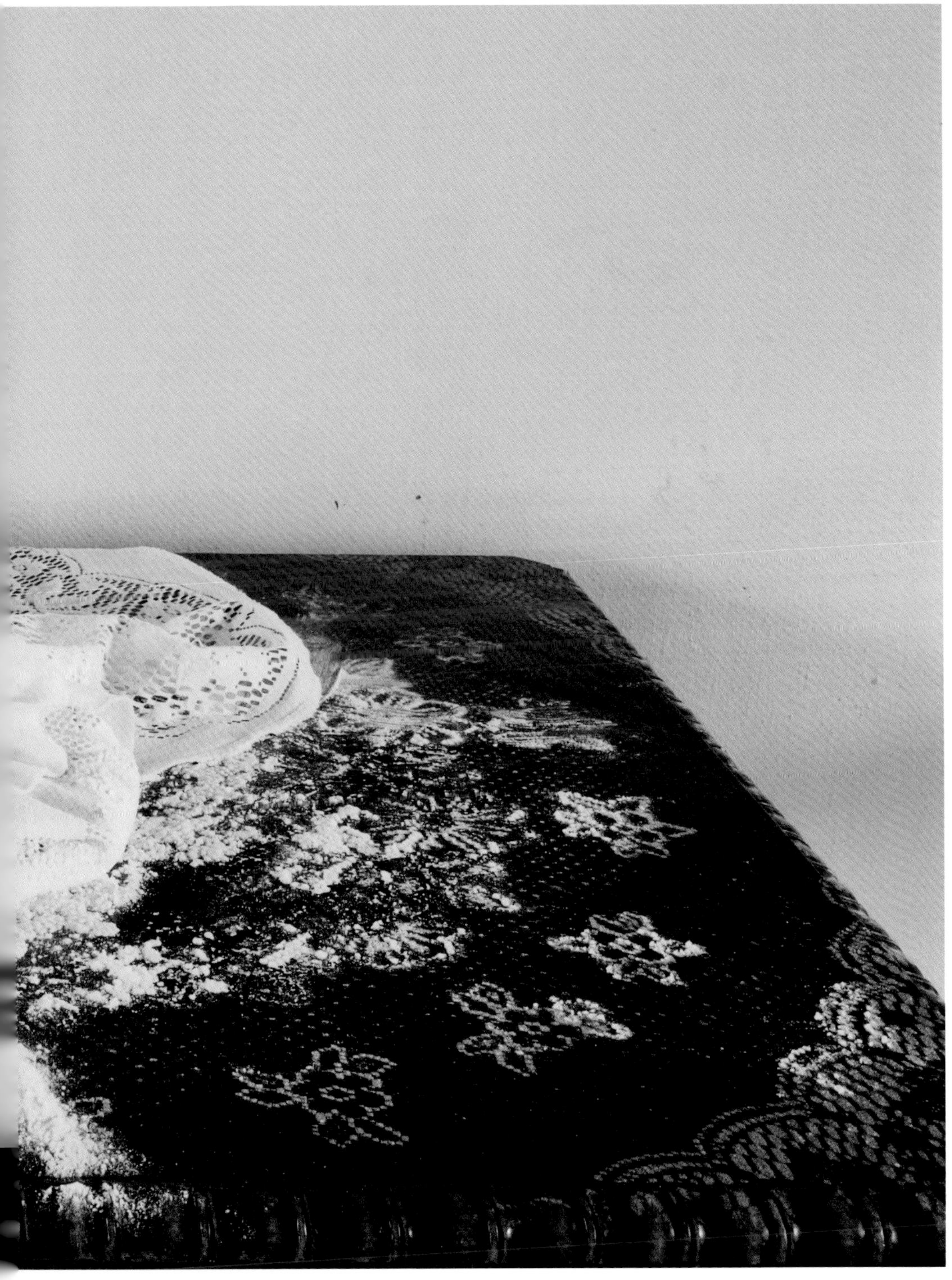

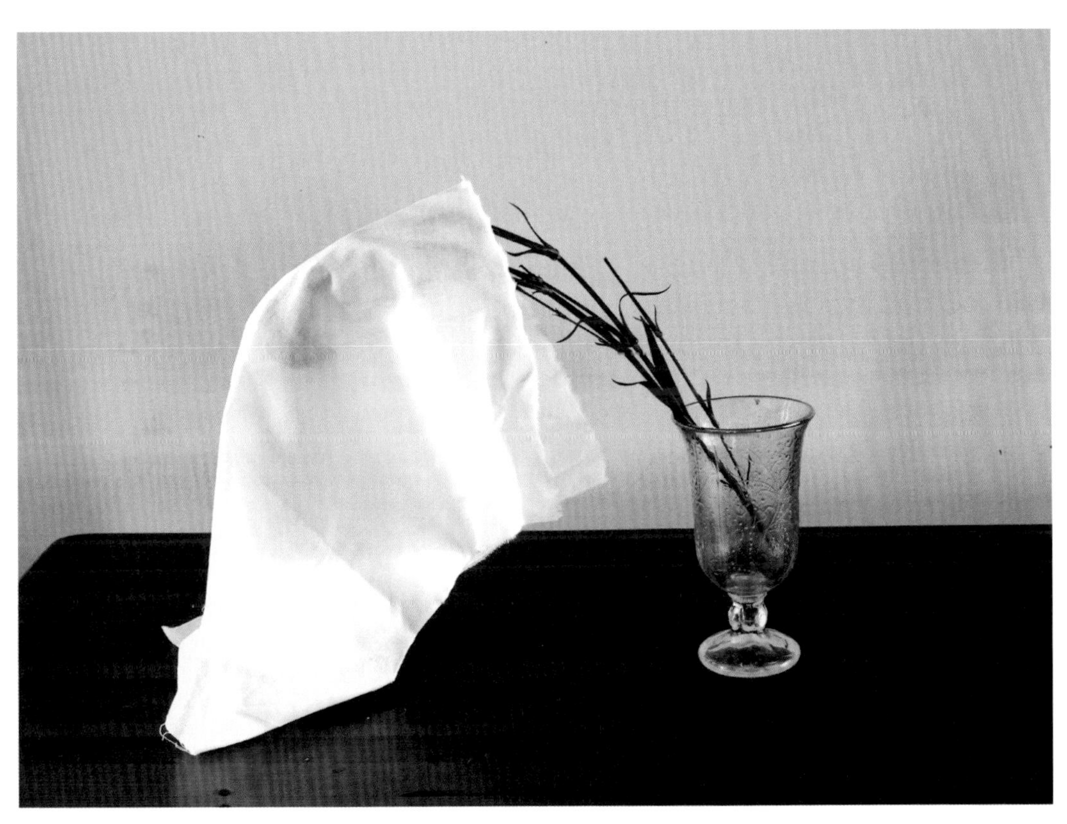

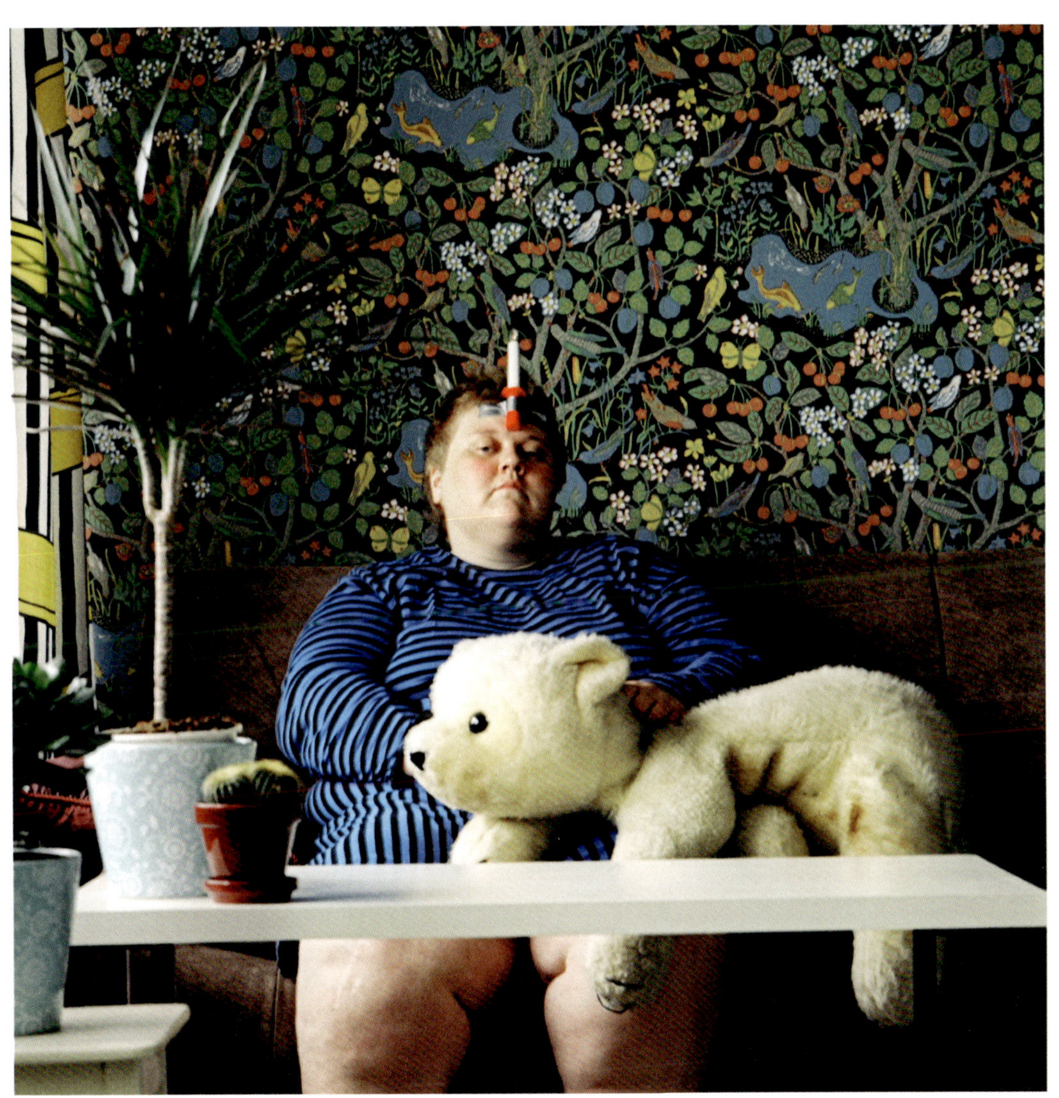

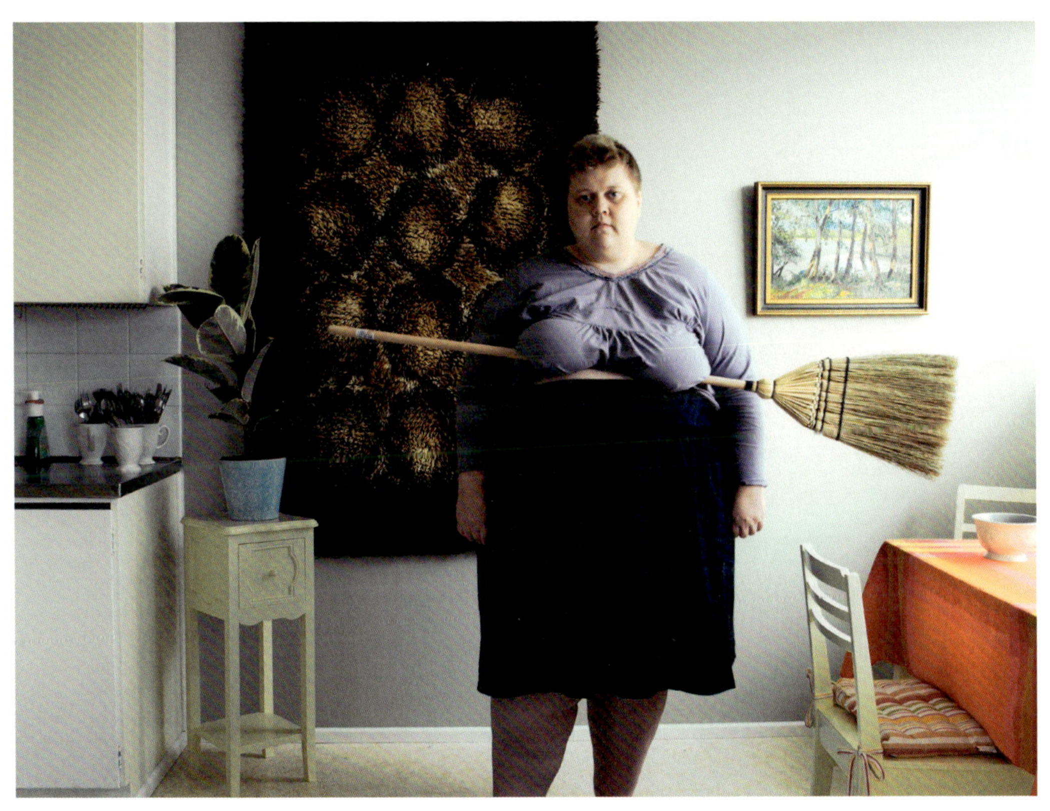

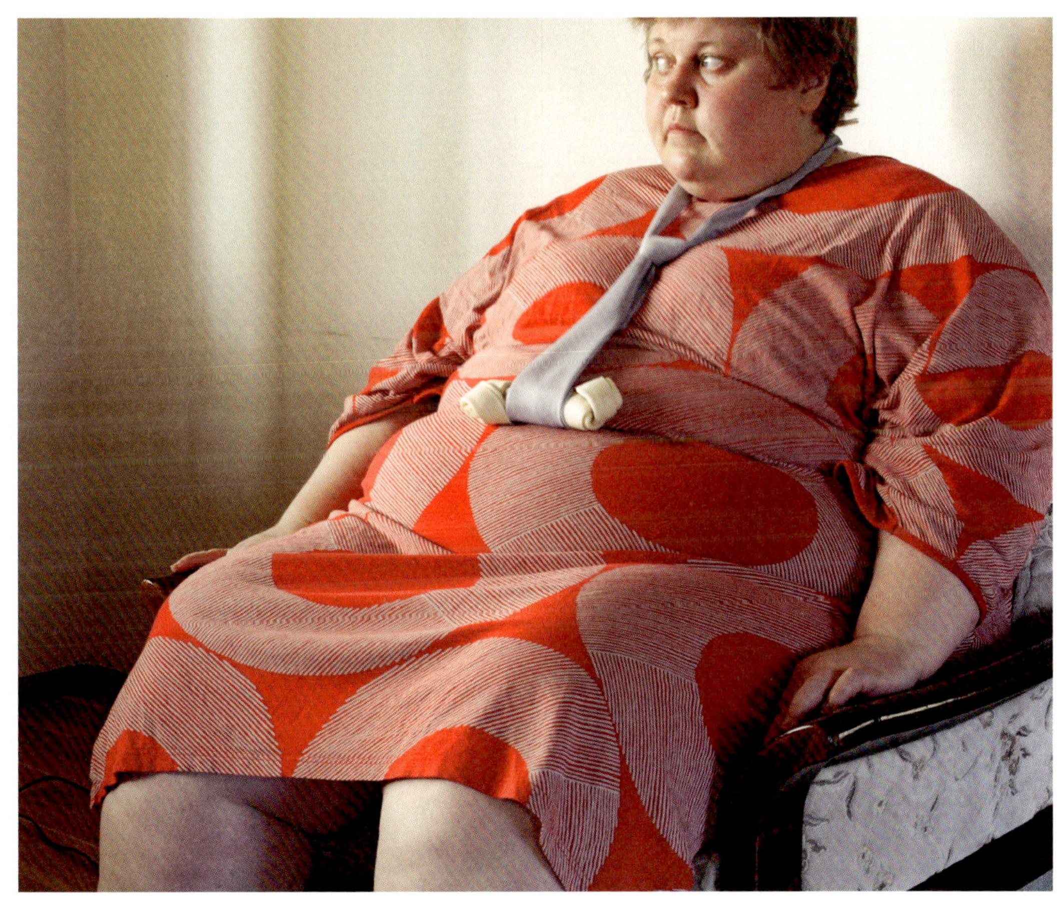

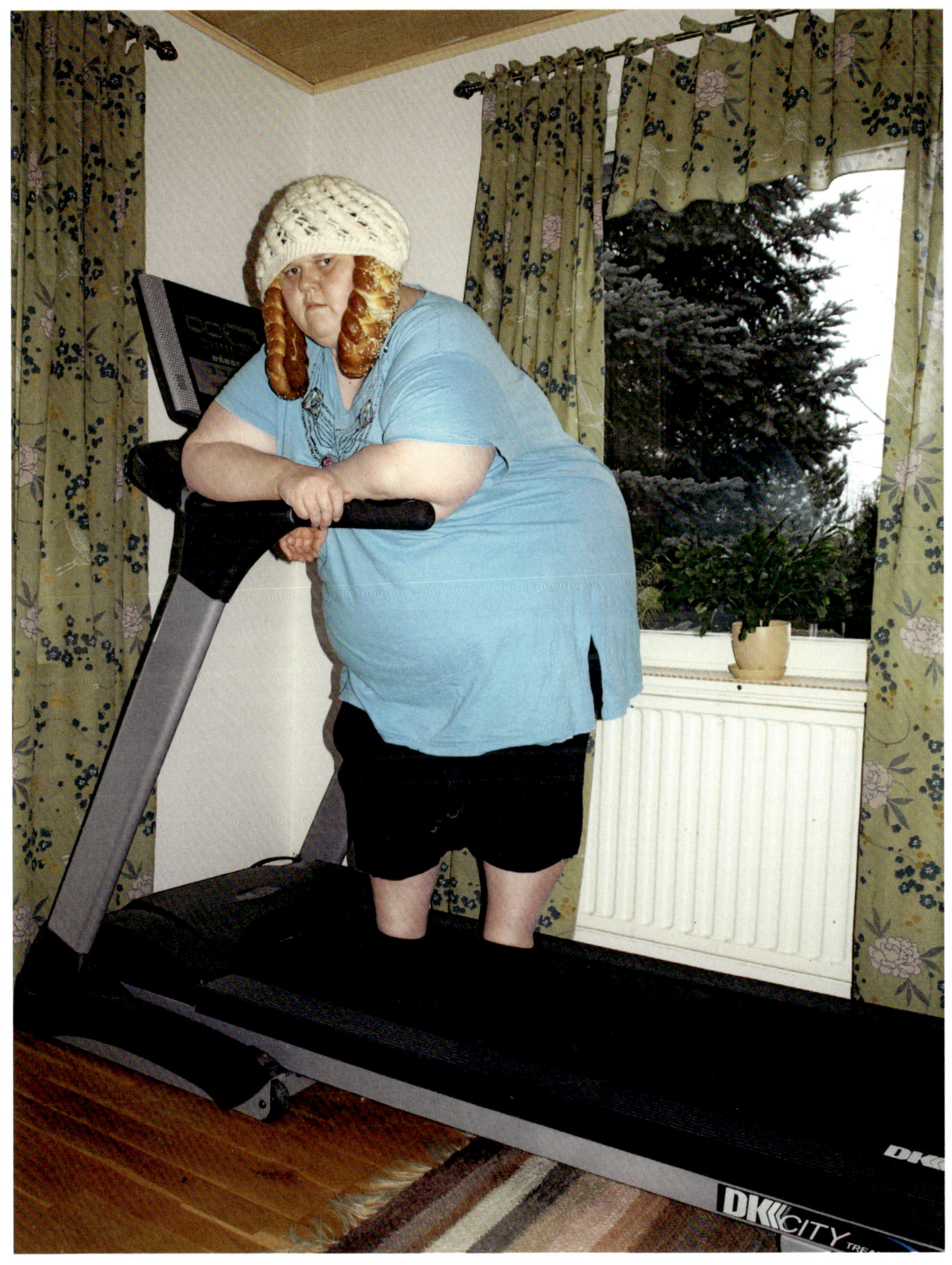

DK CITY TRE

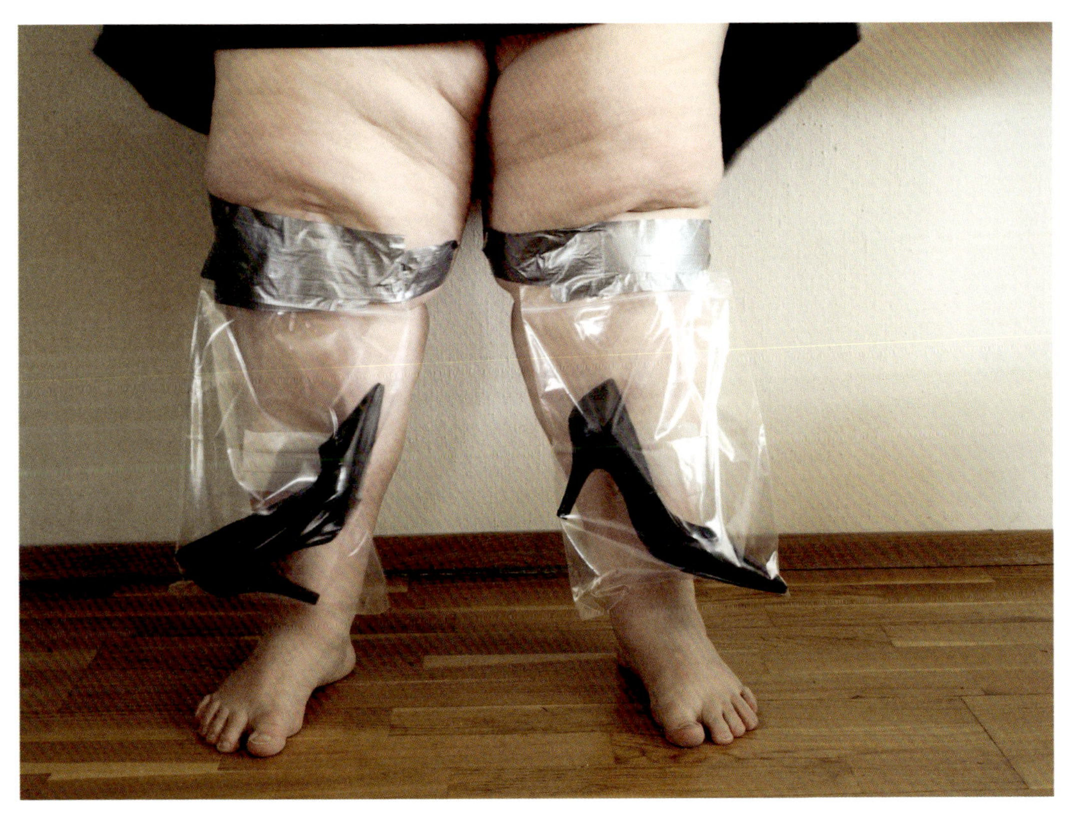

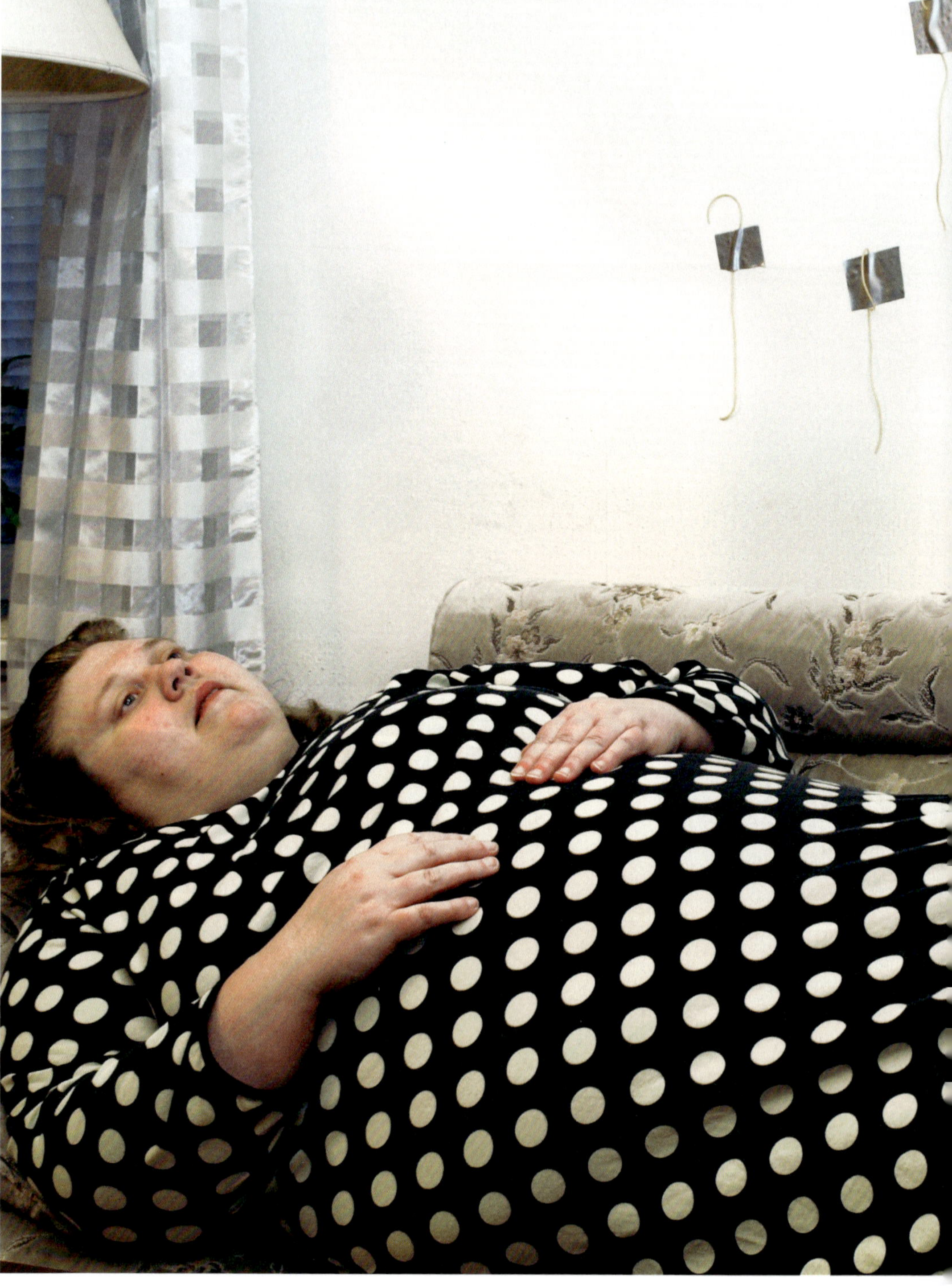

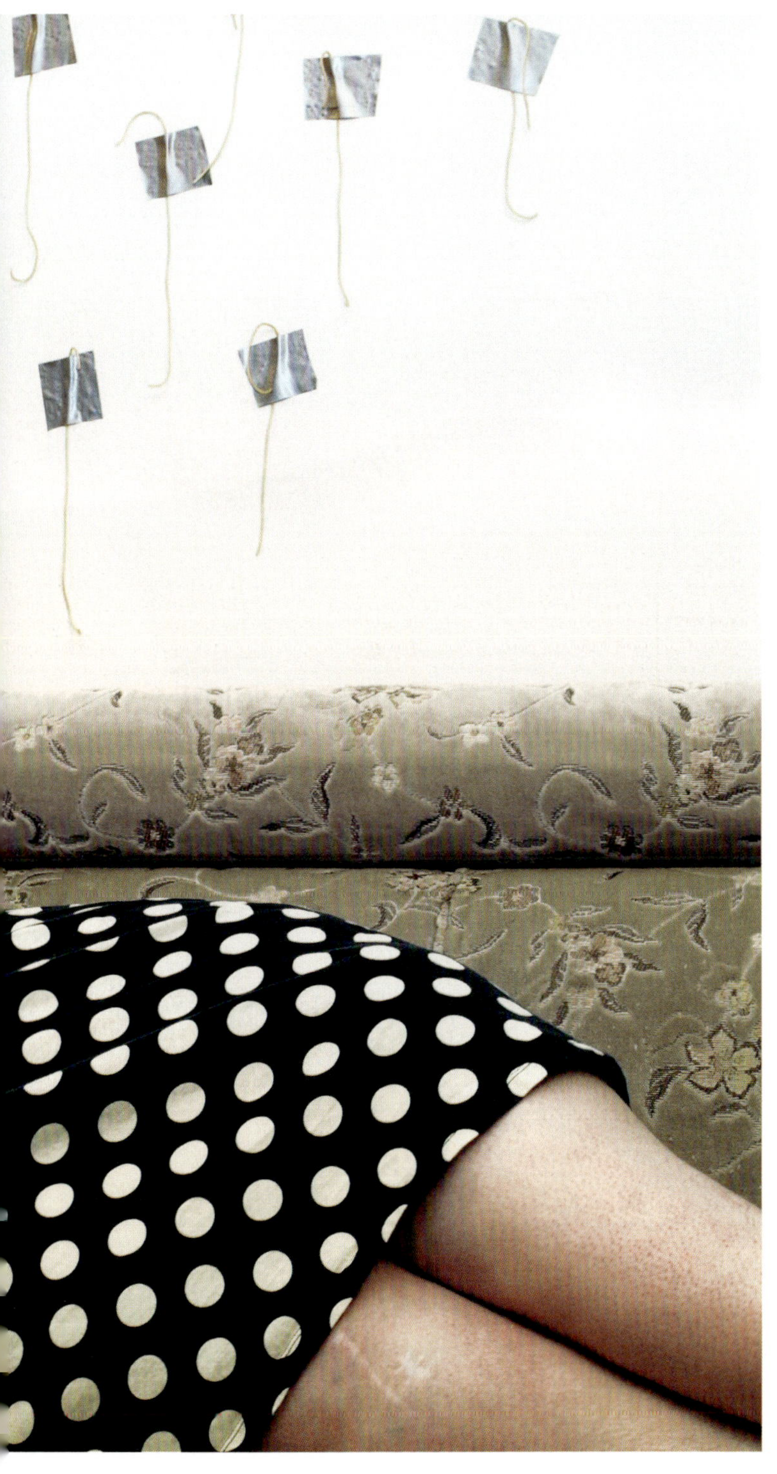

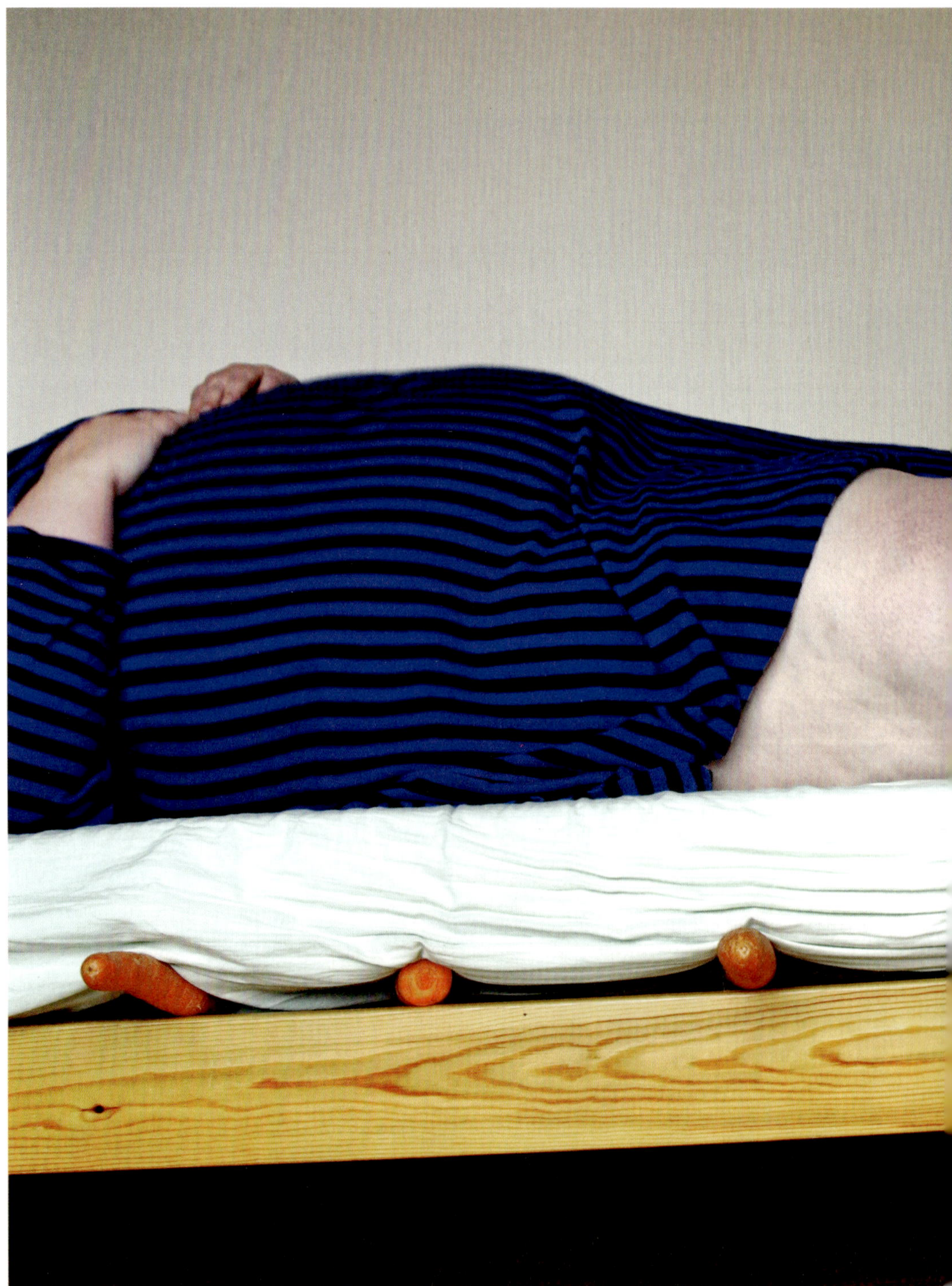

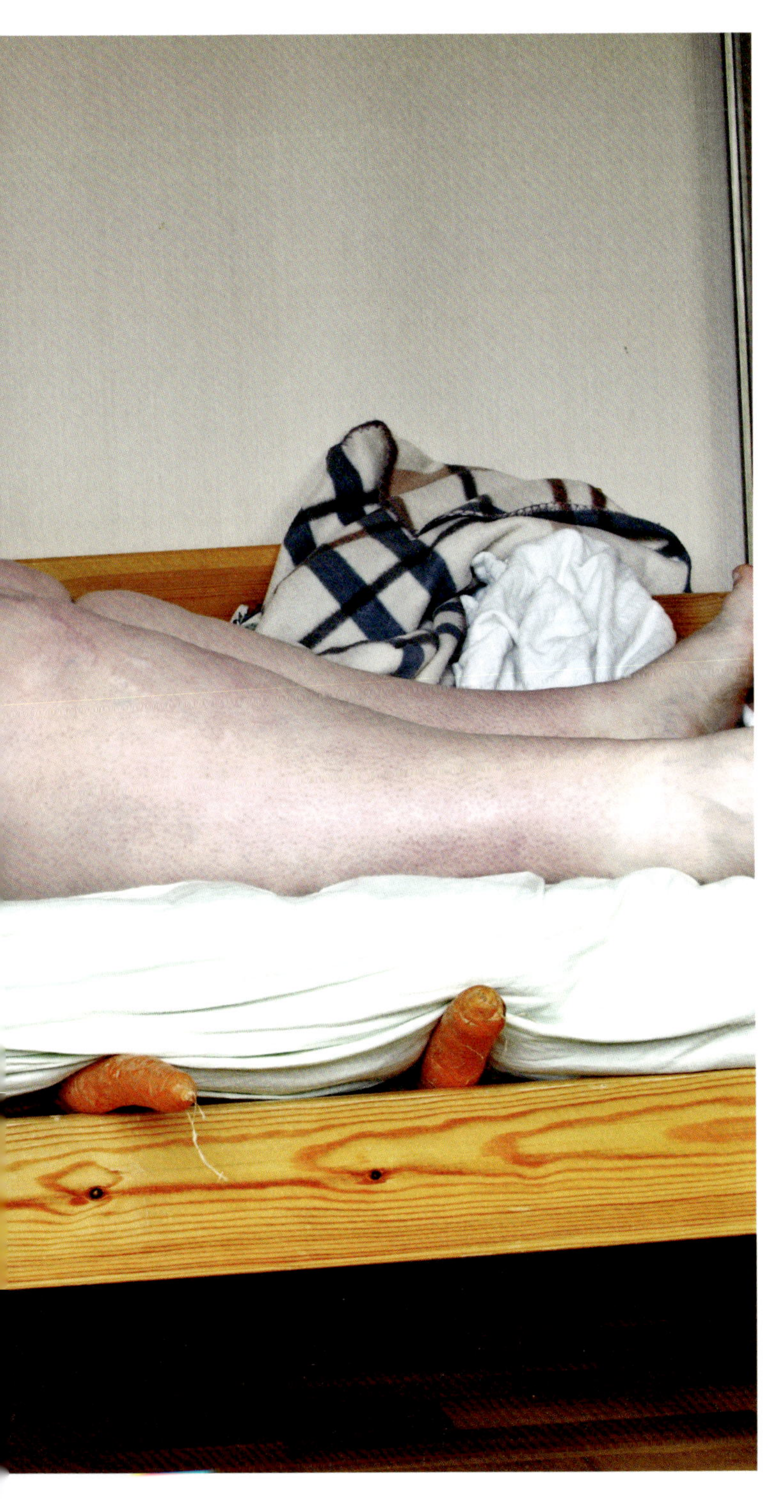

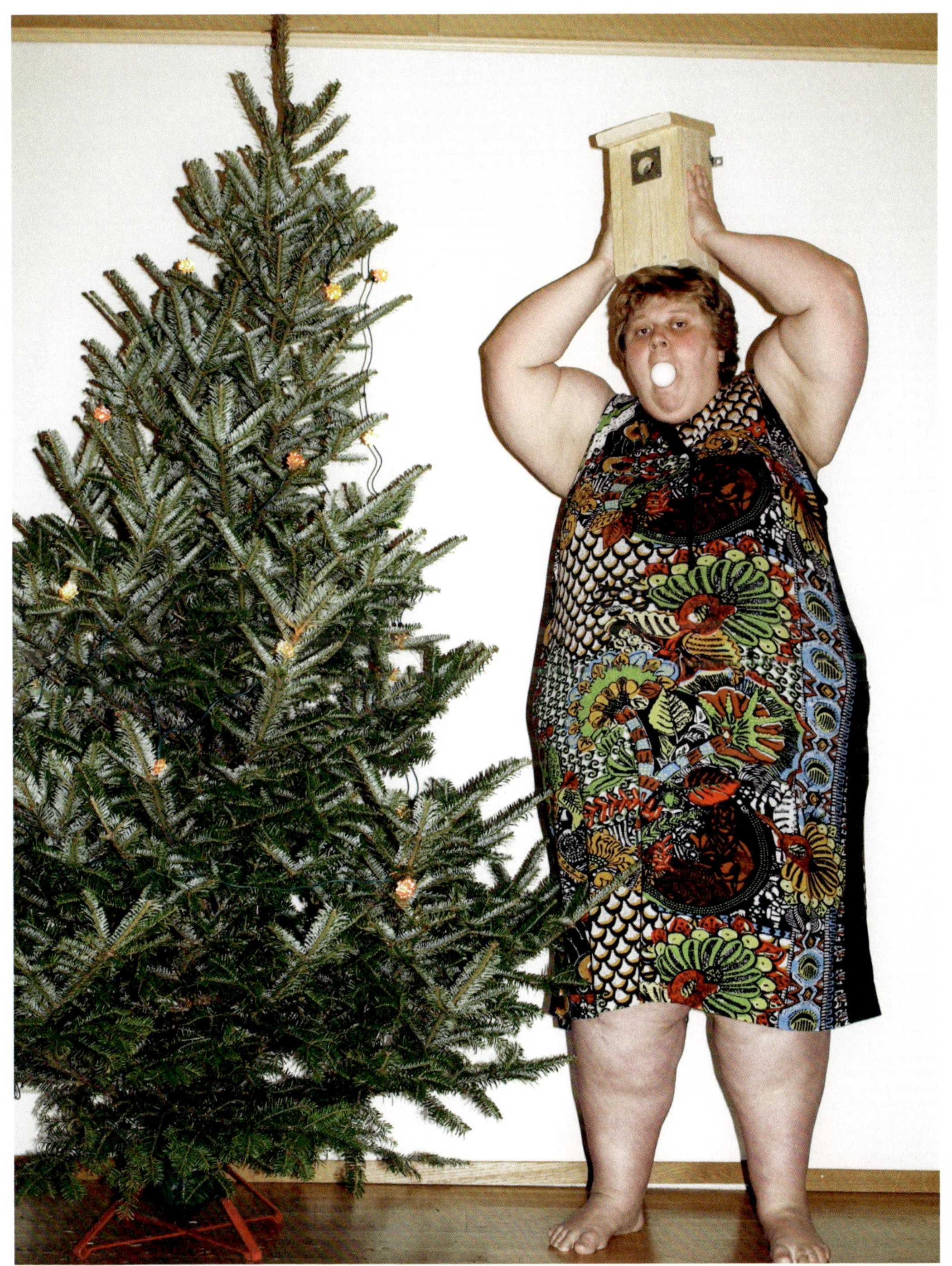

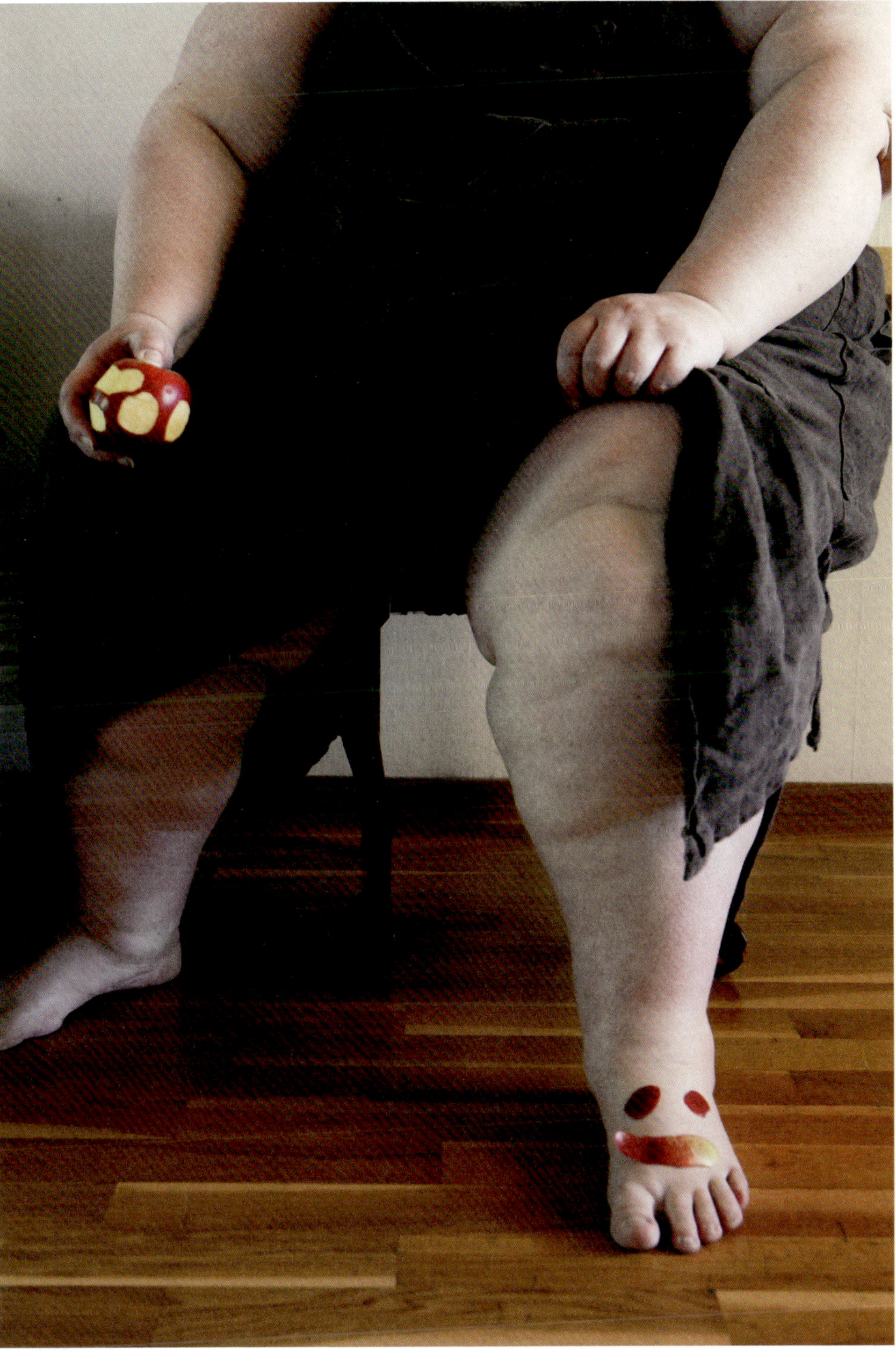

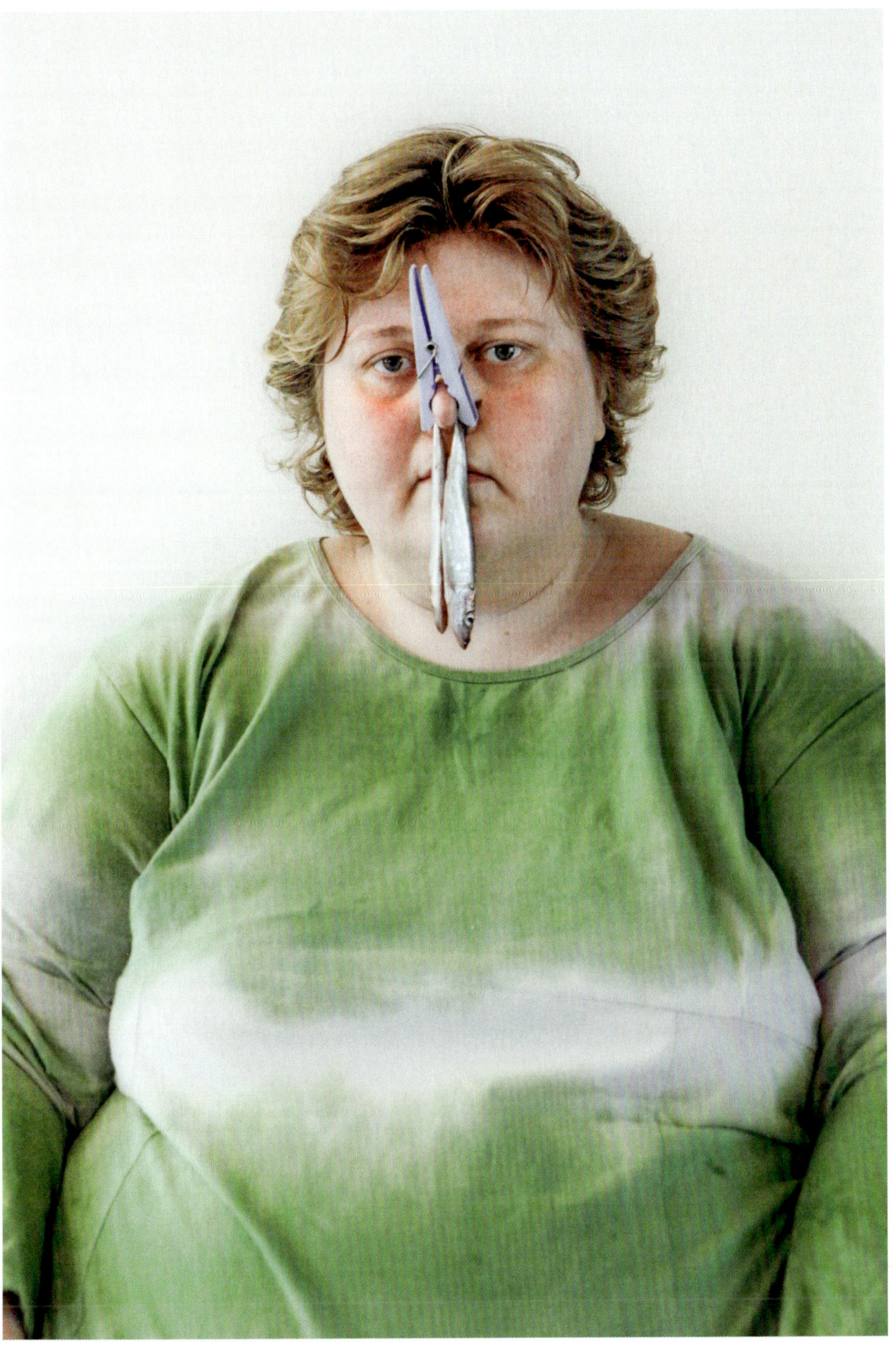

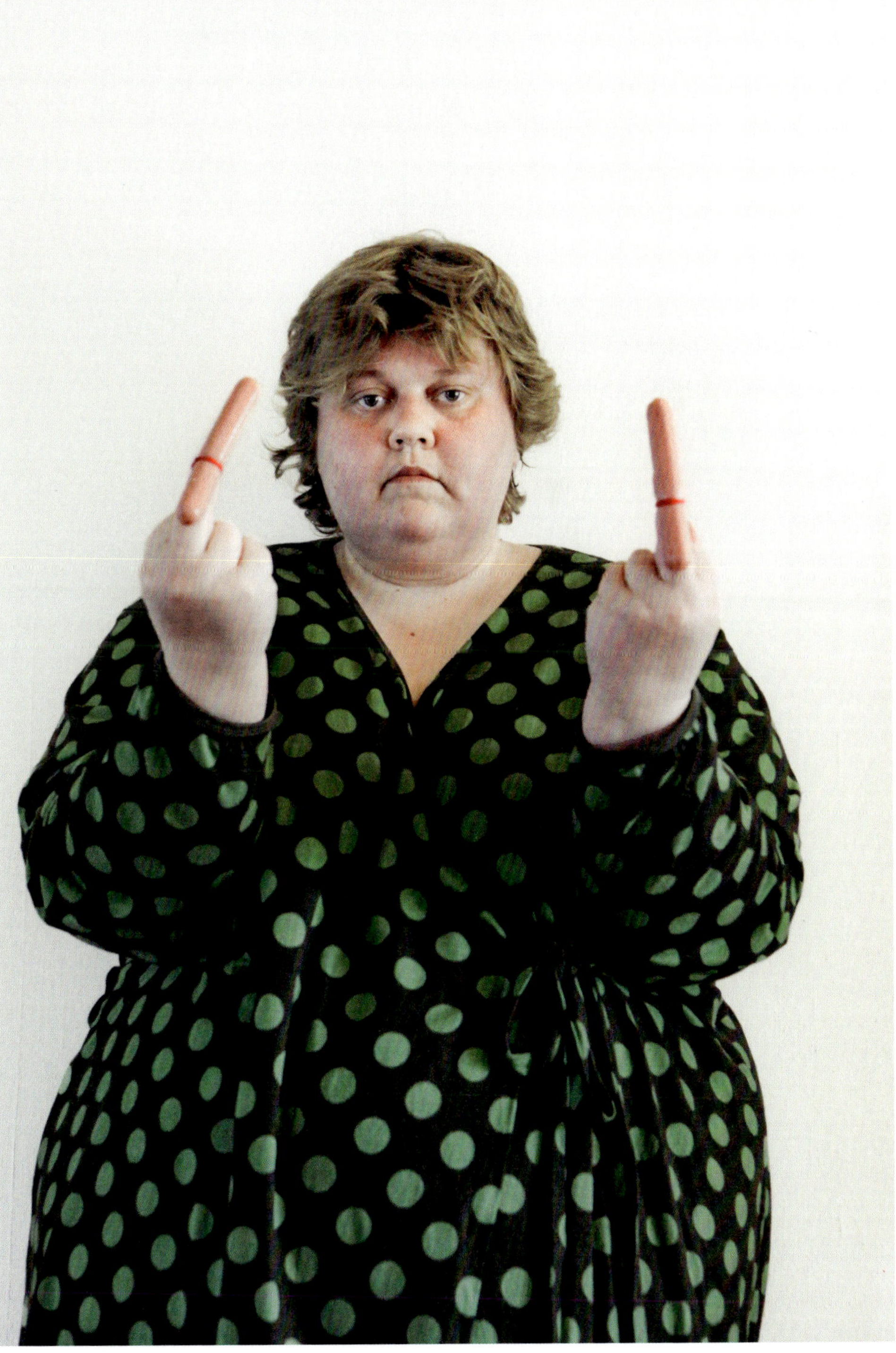

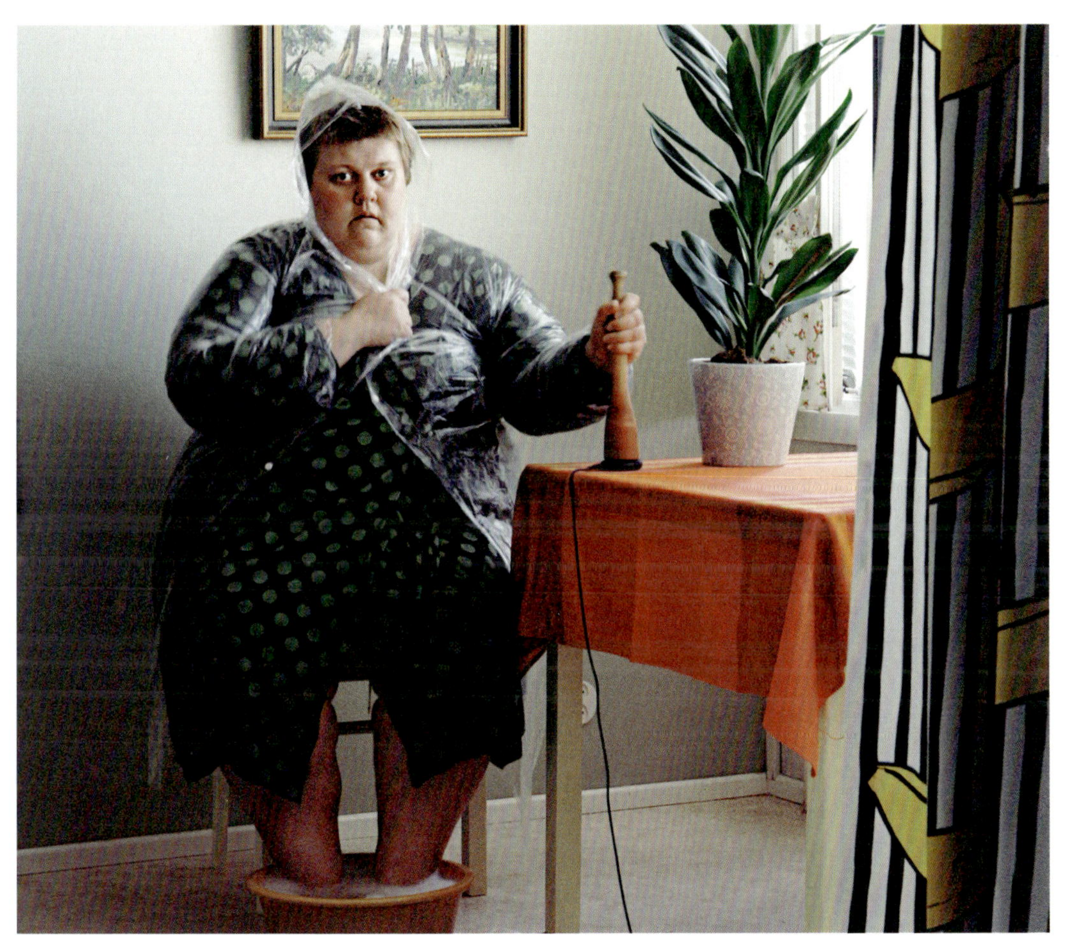

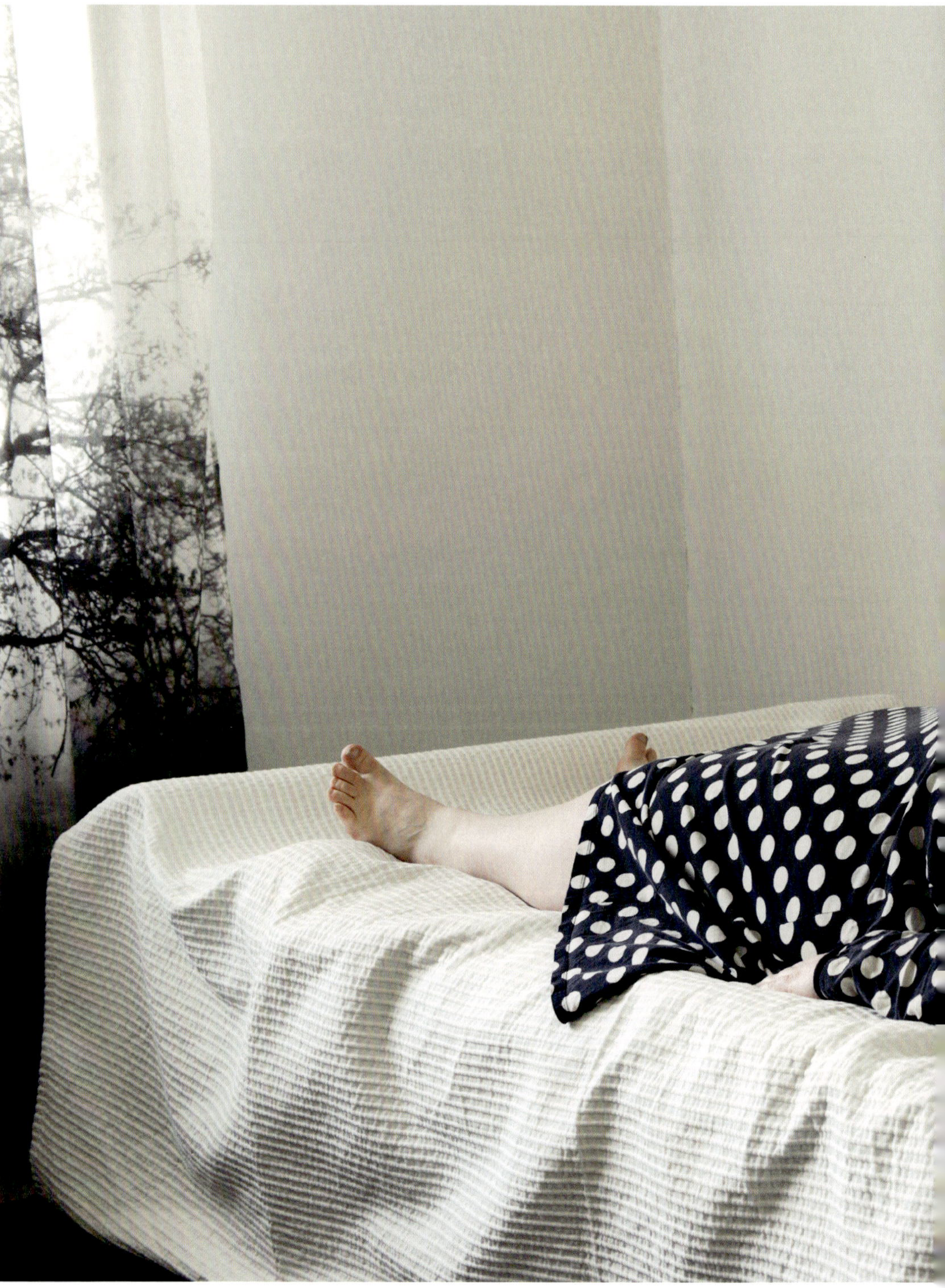

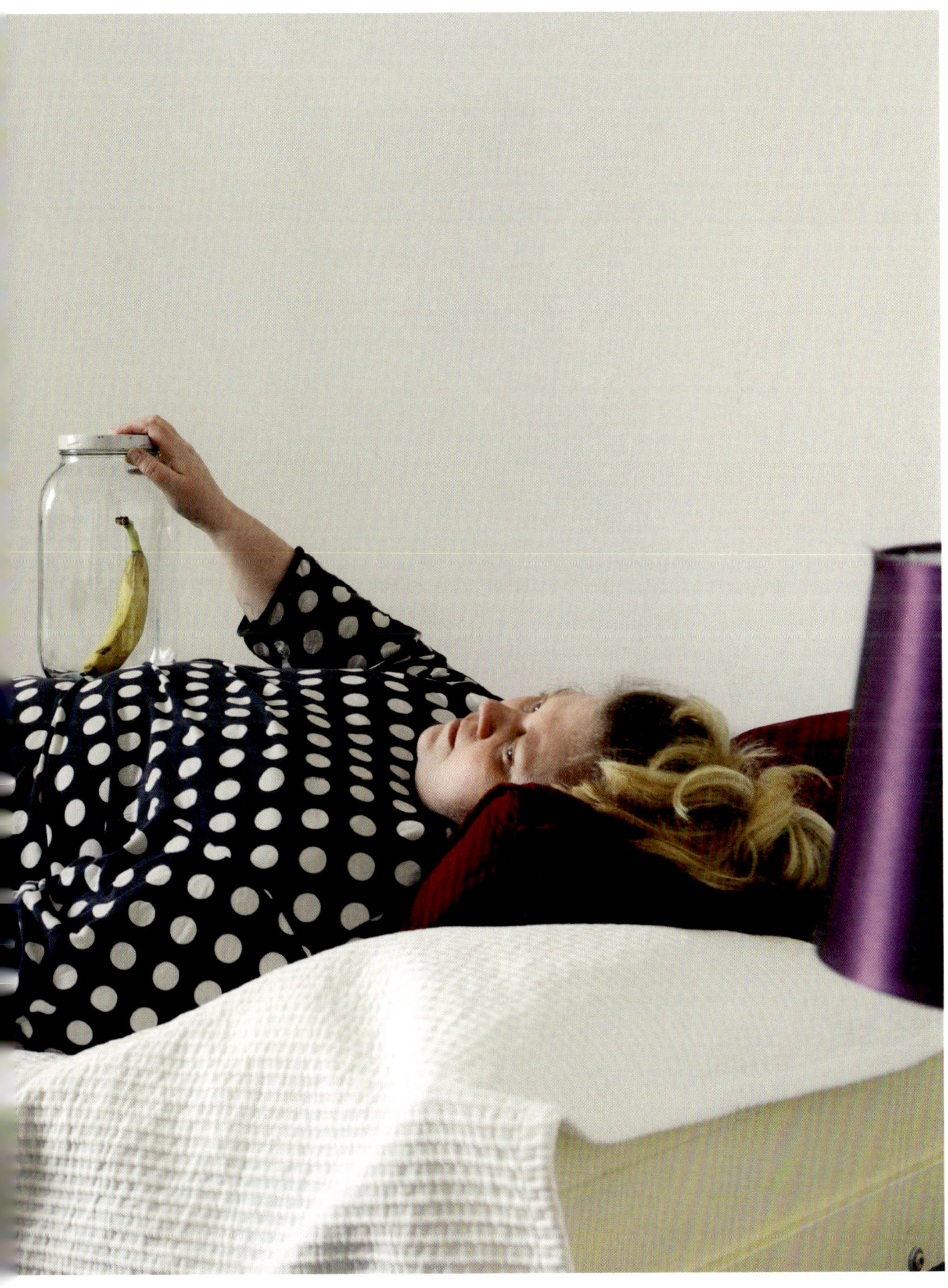

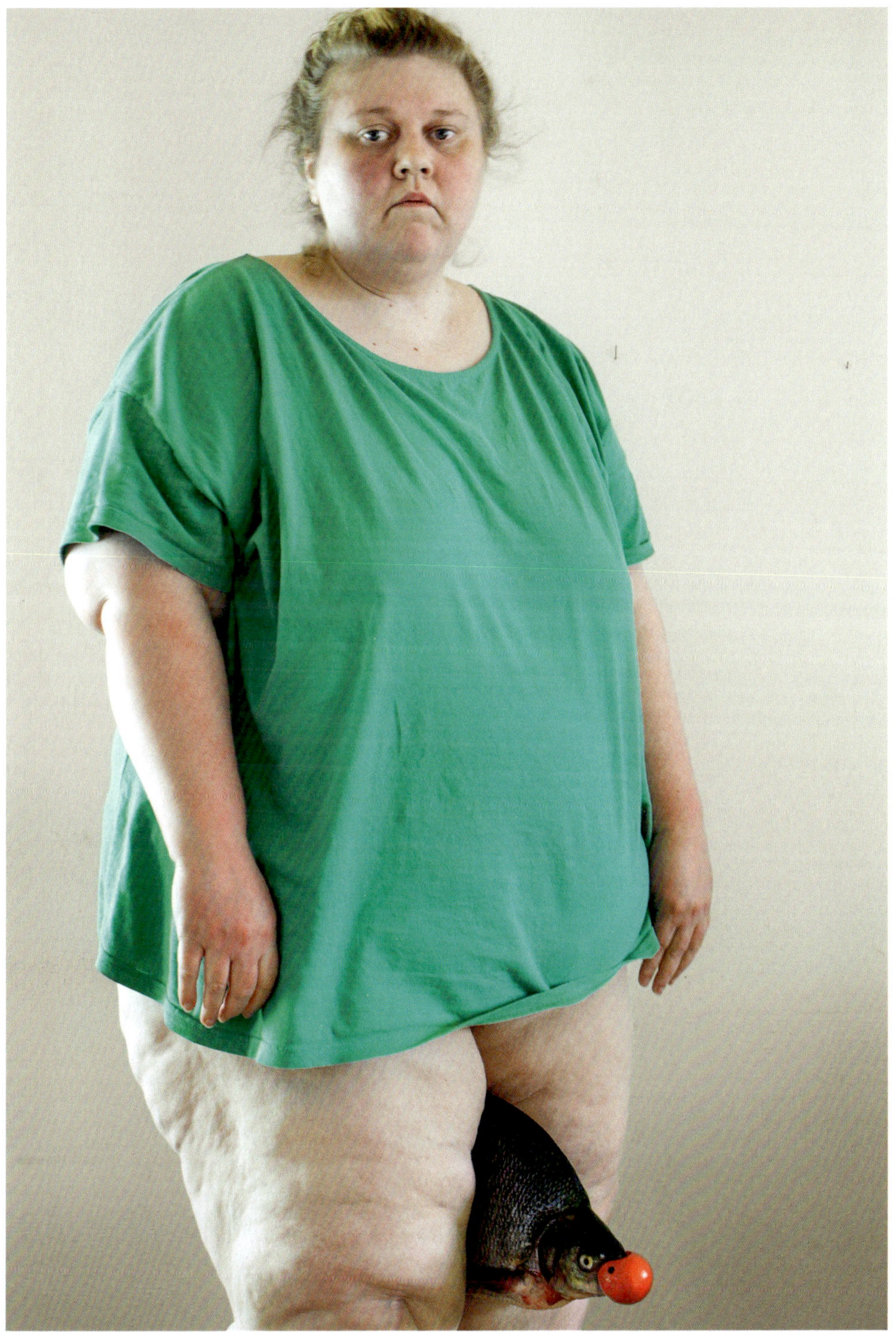

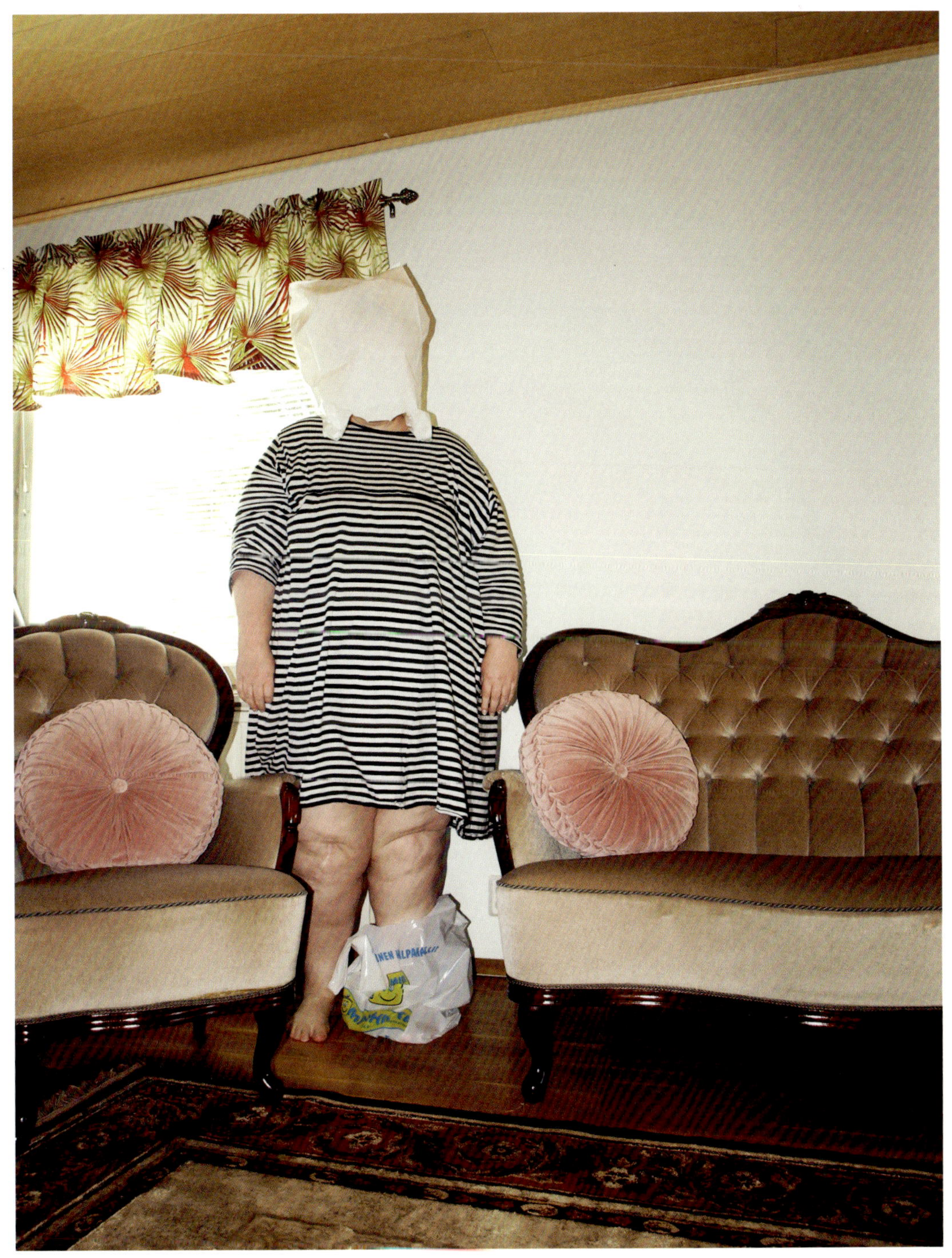

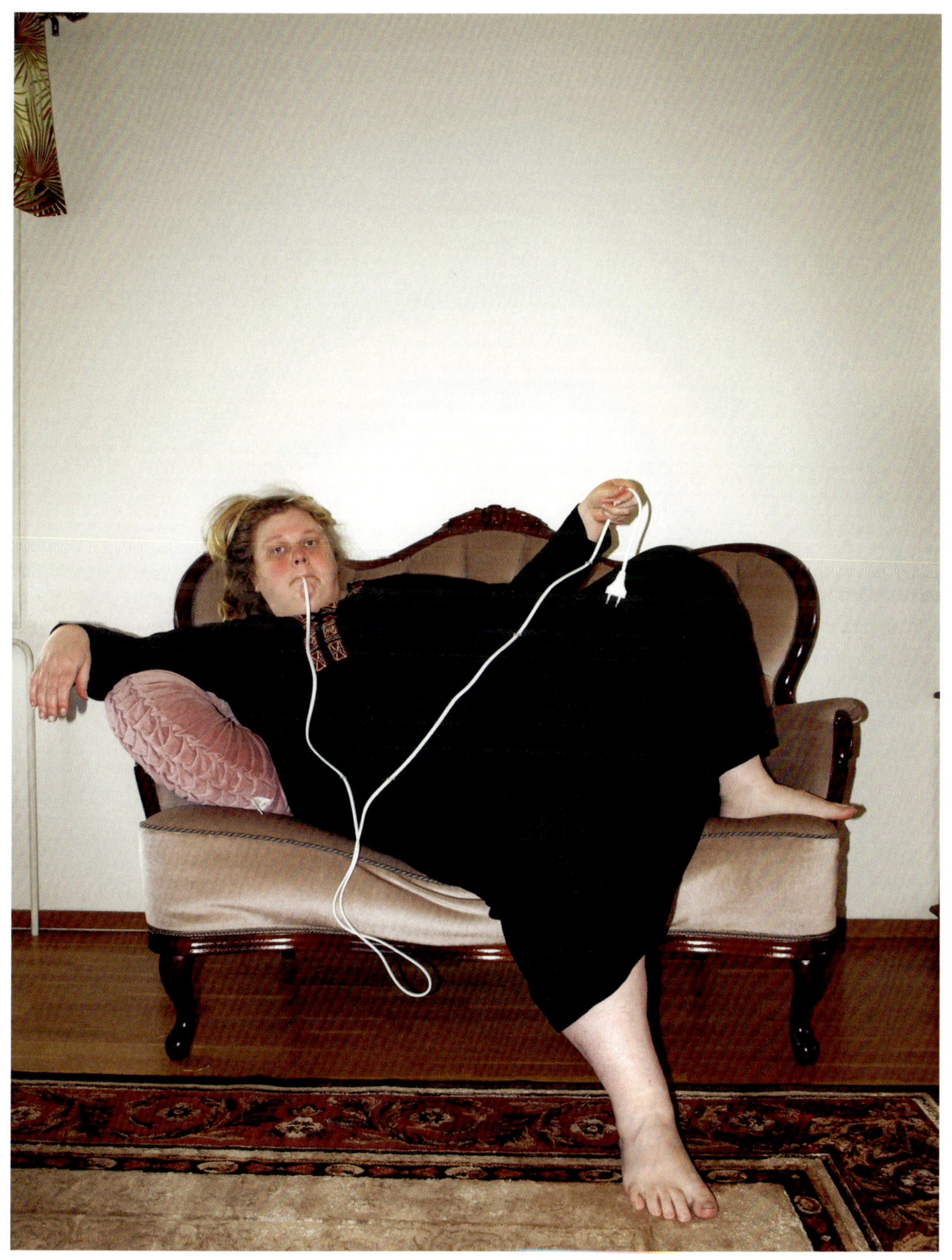

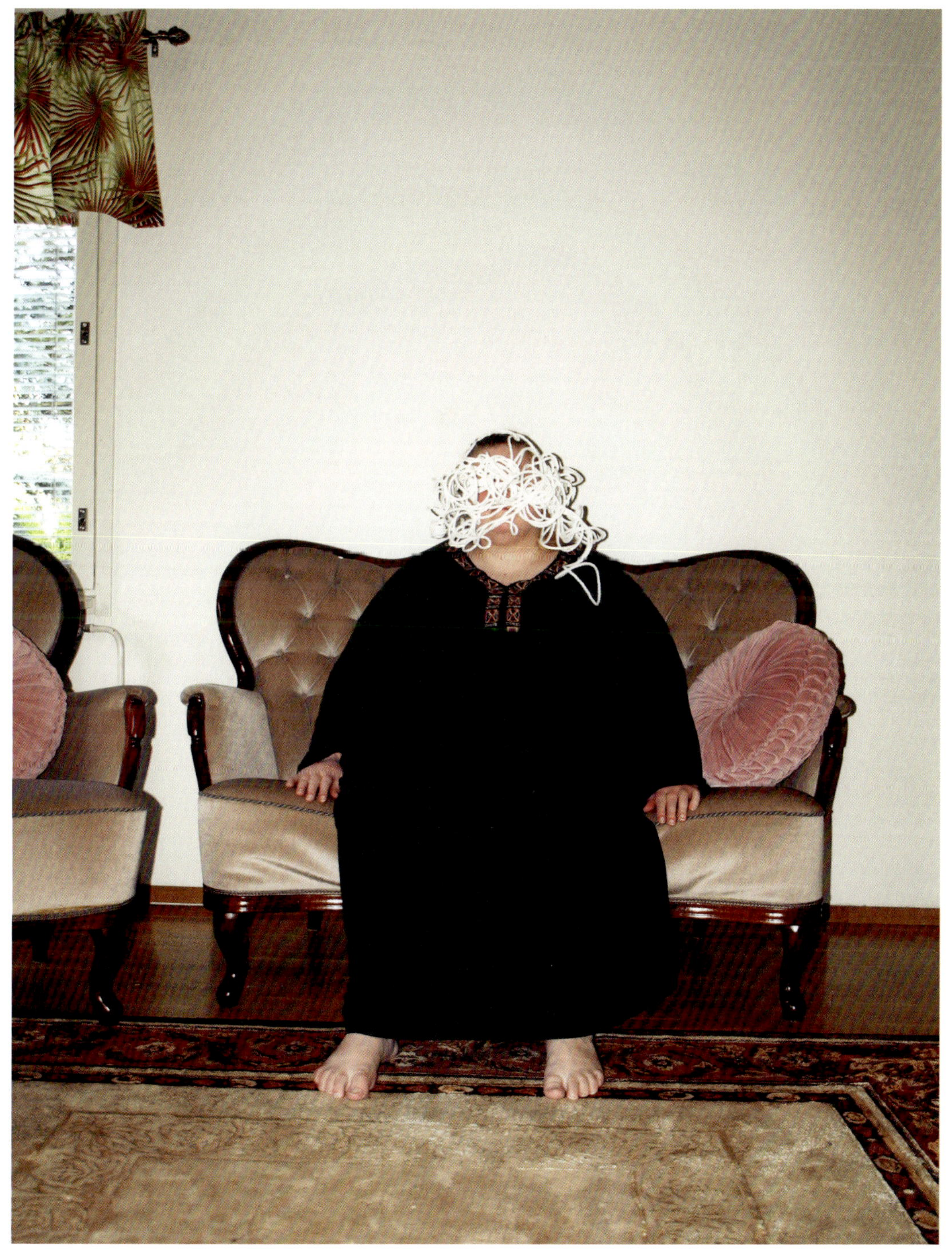

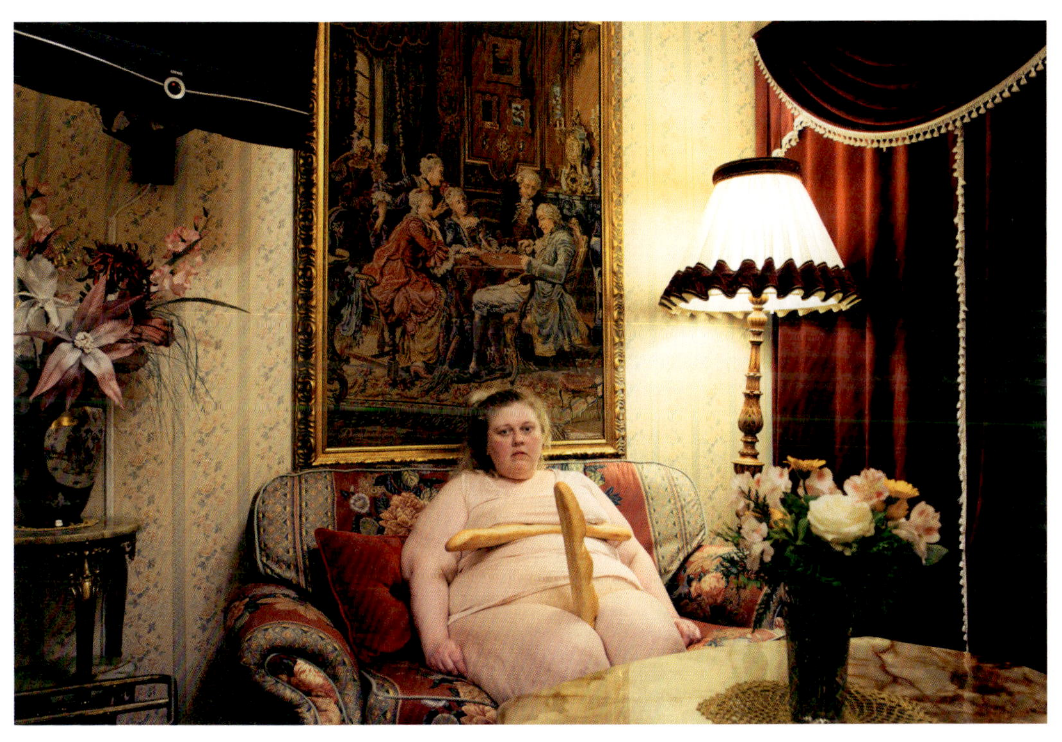

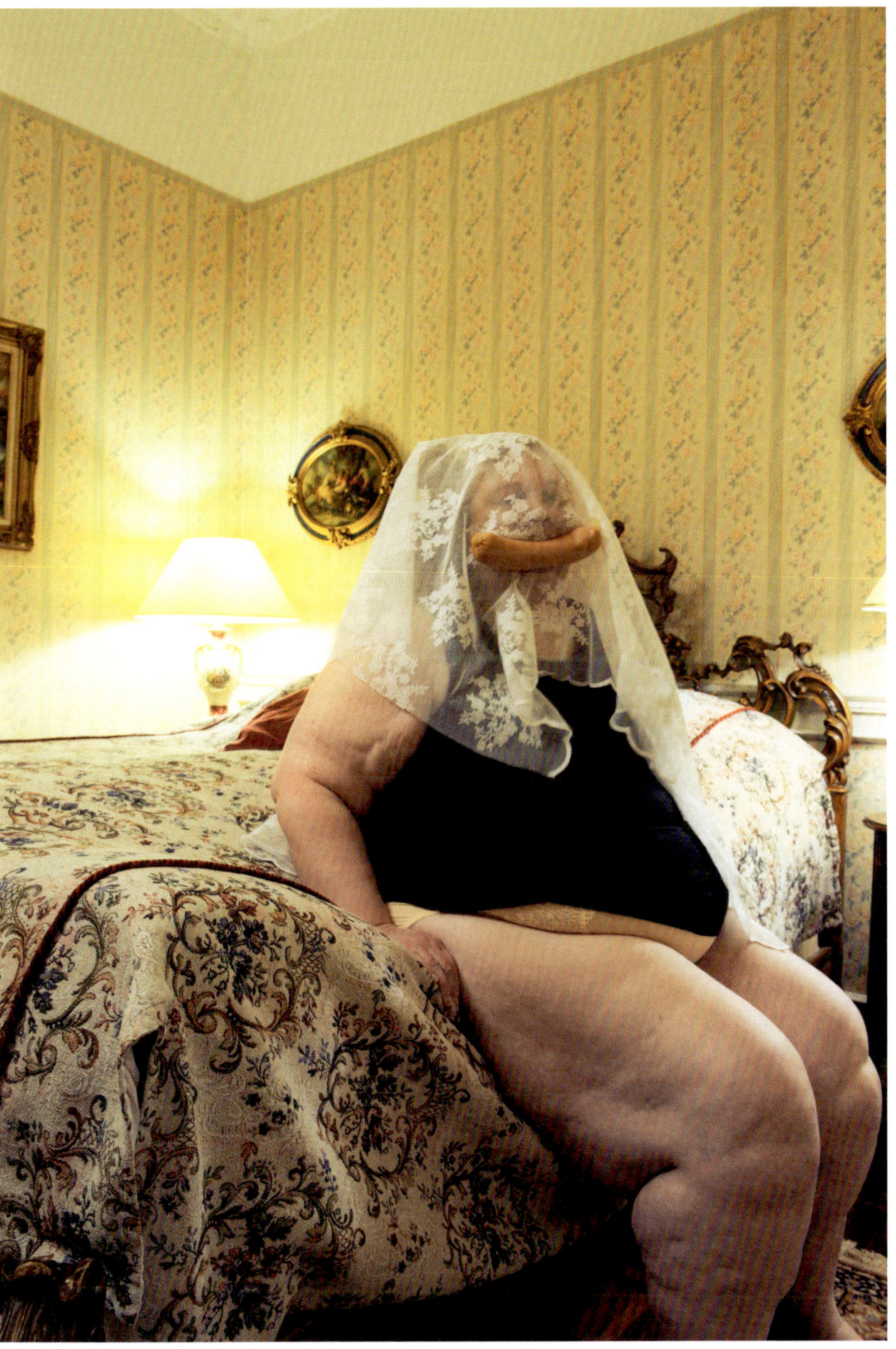

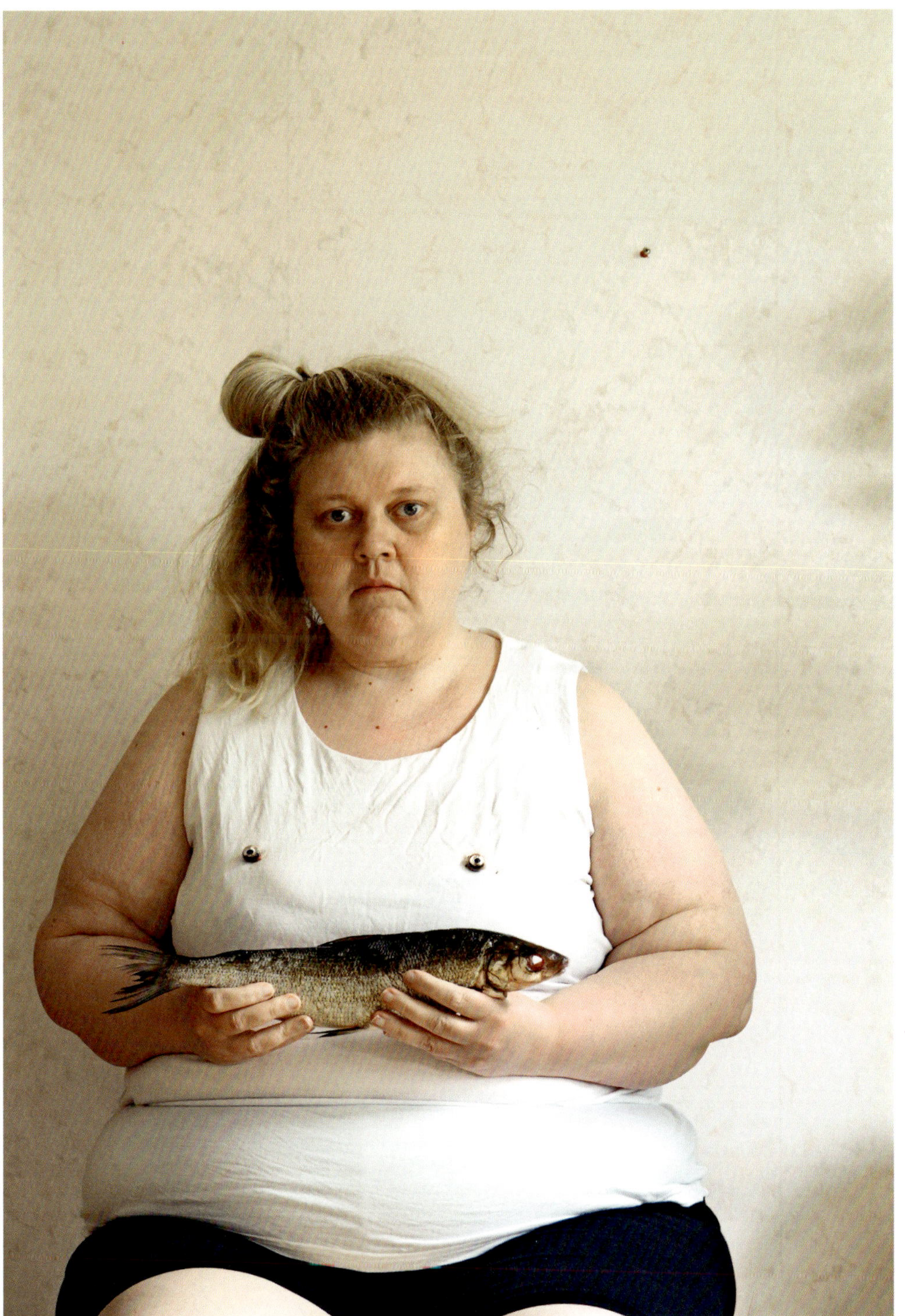

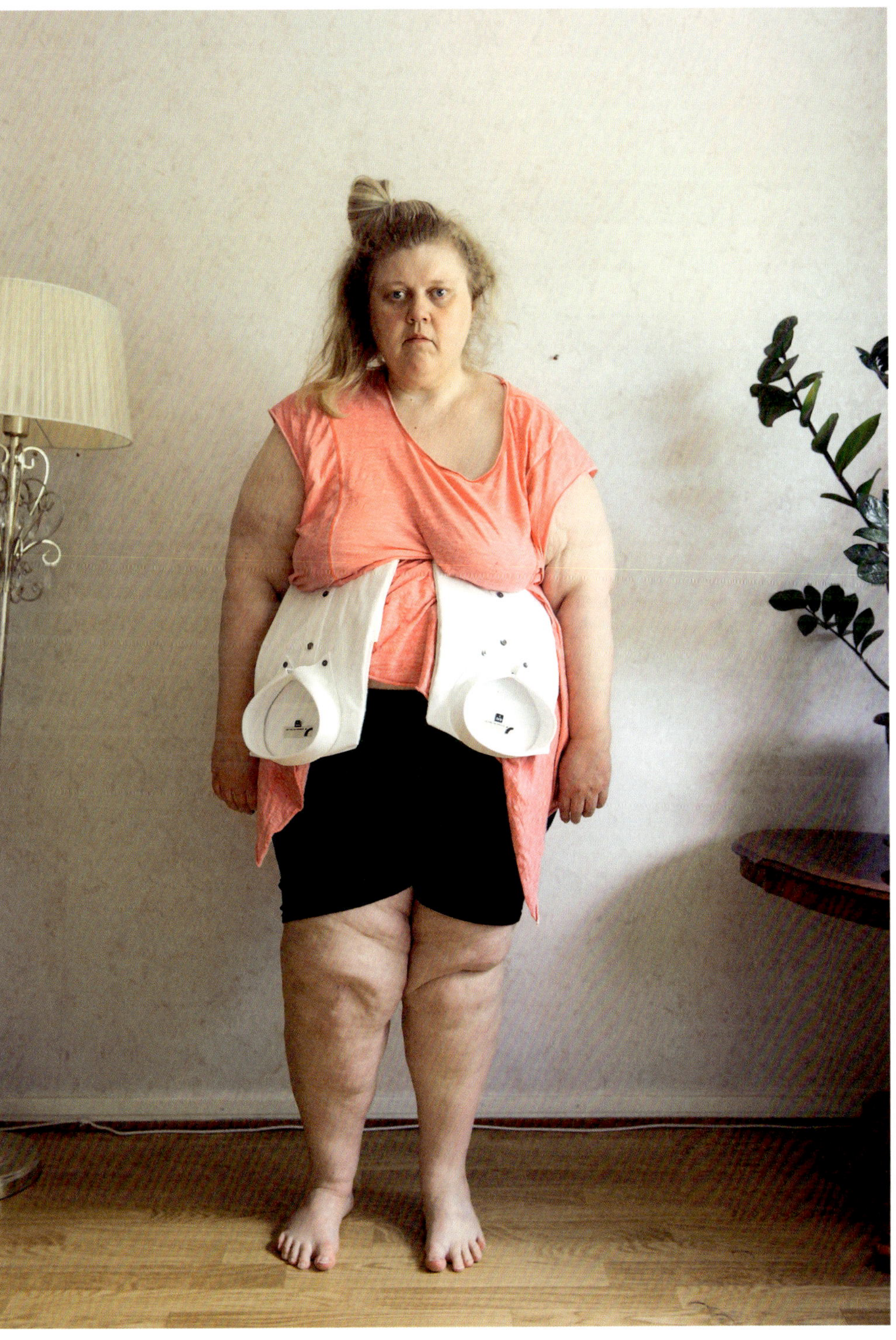

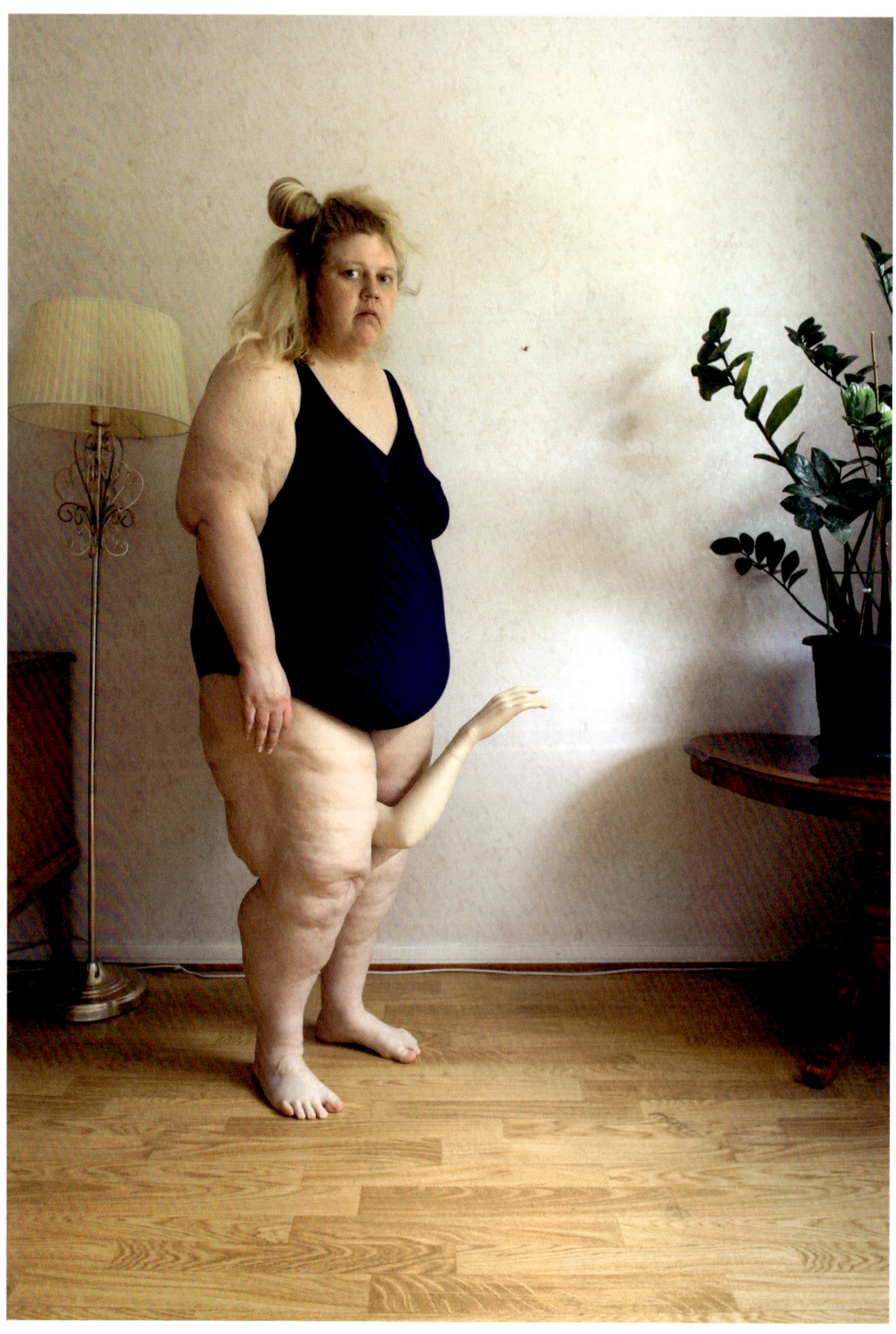

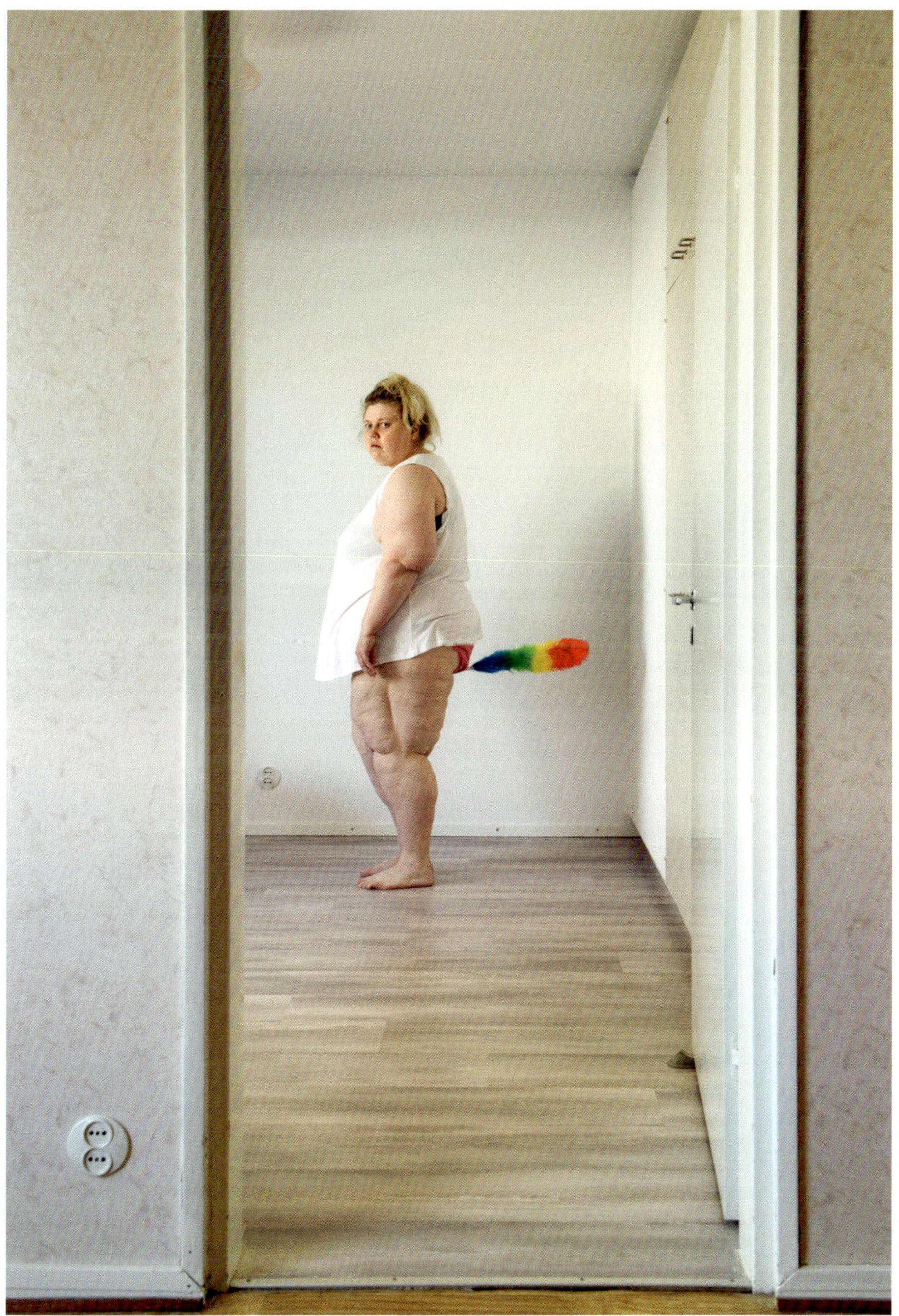

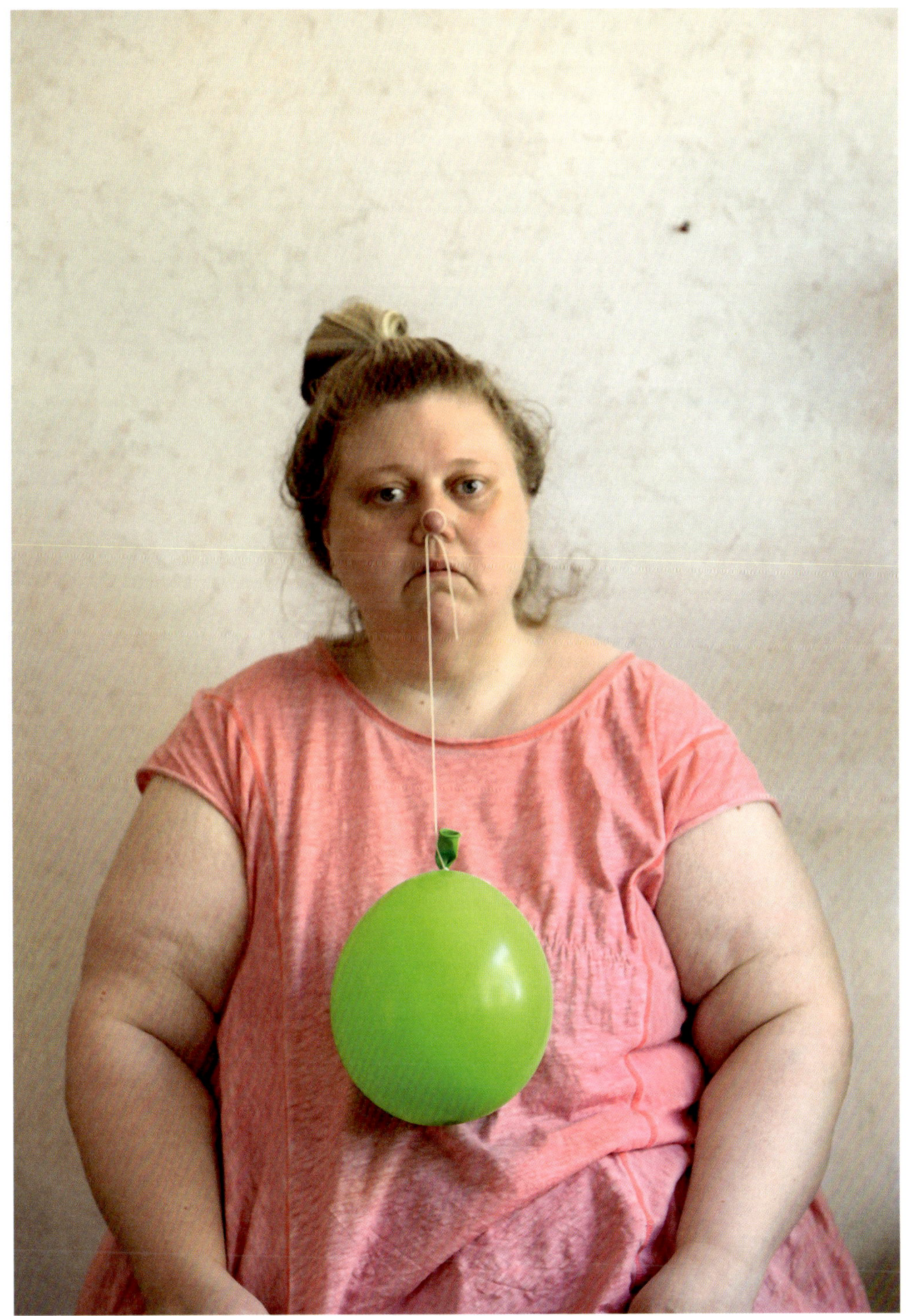

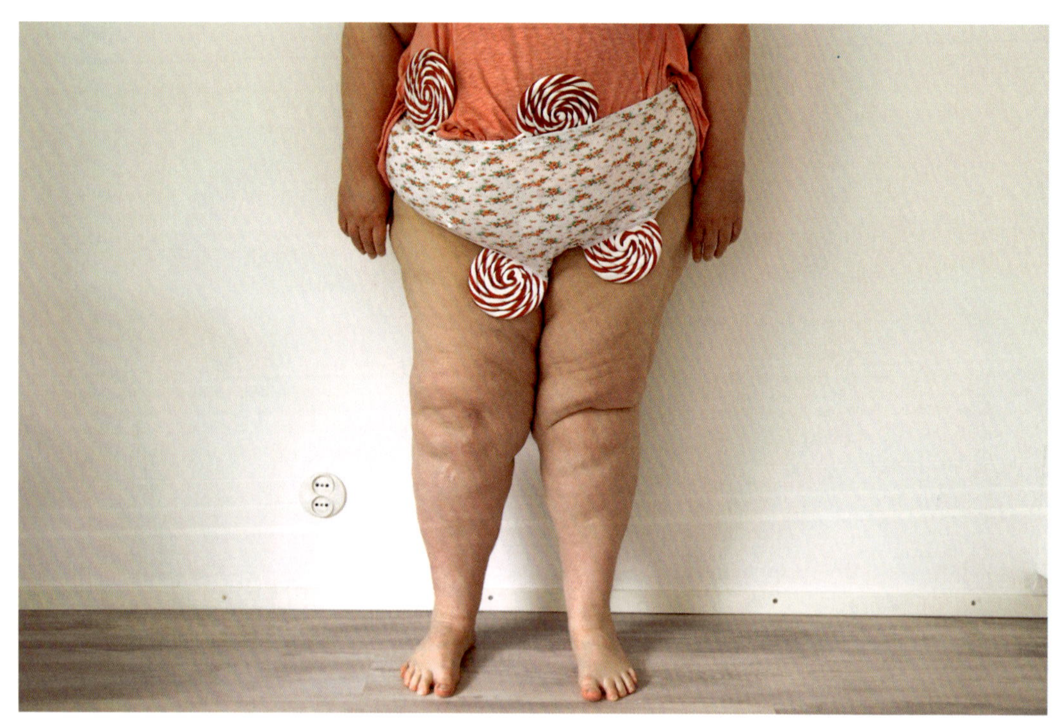

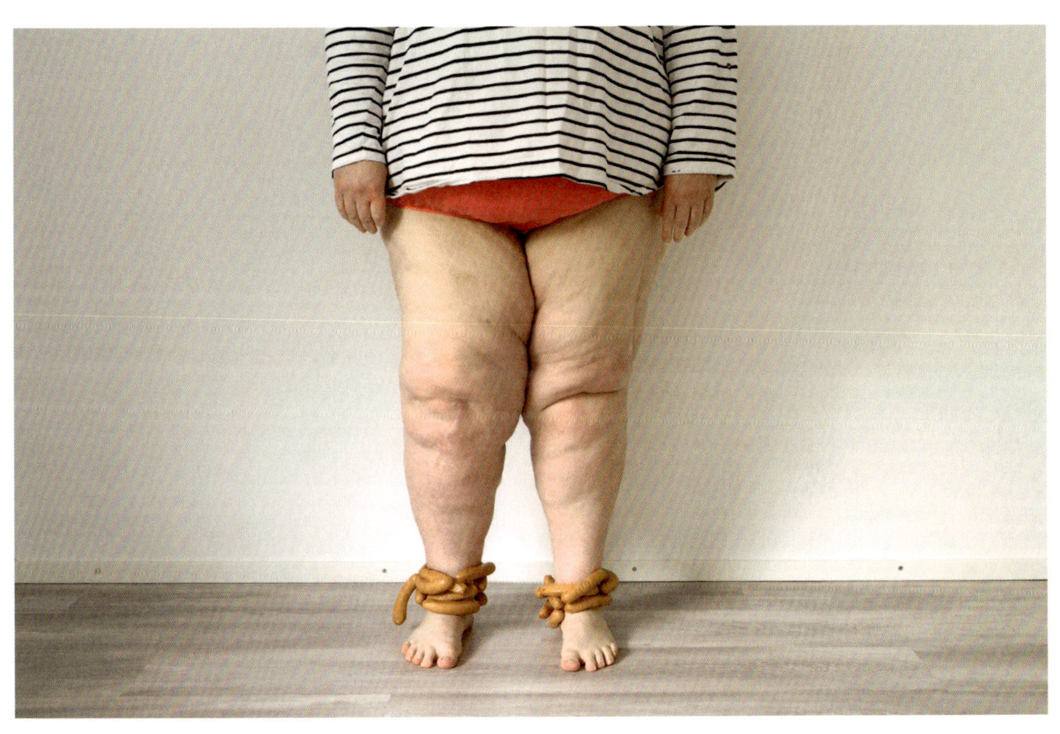

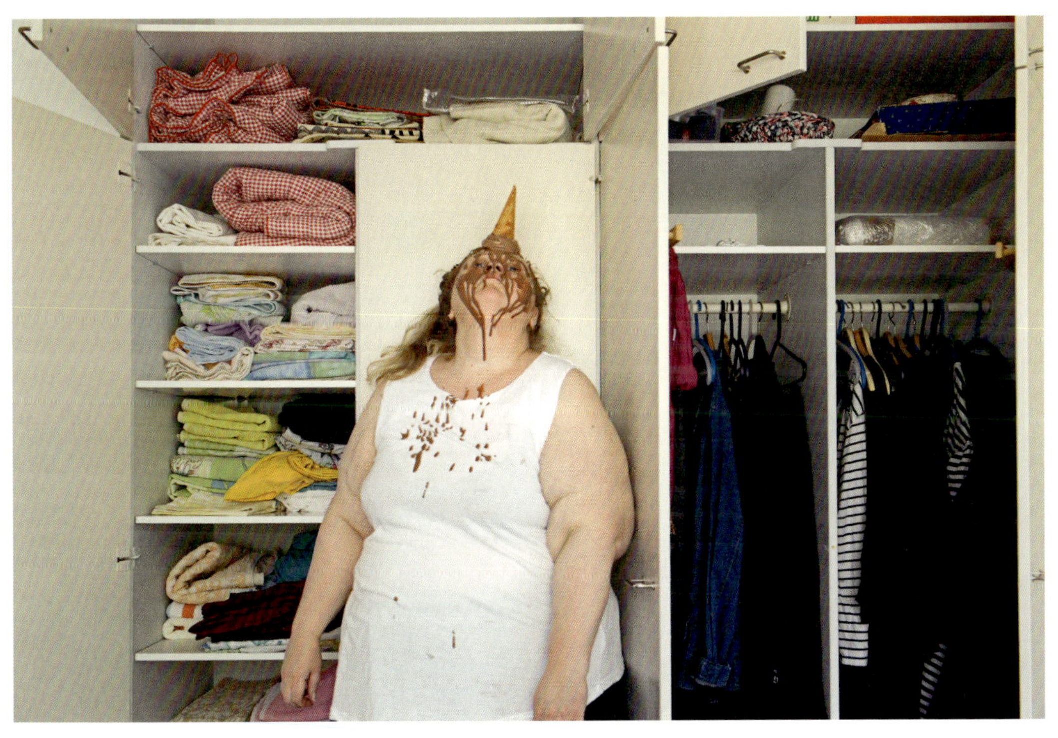

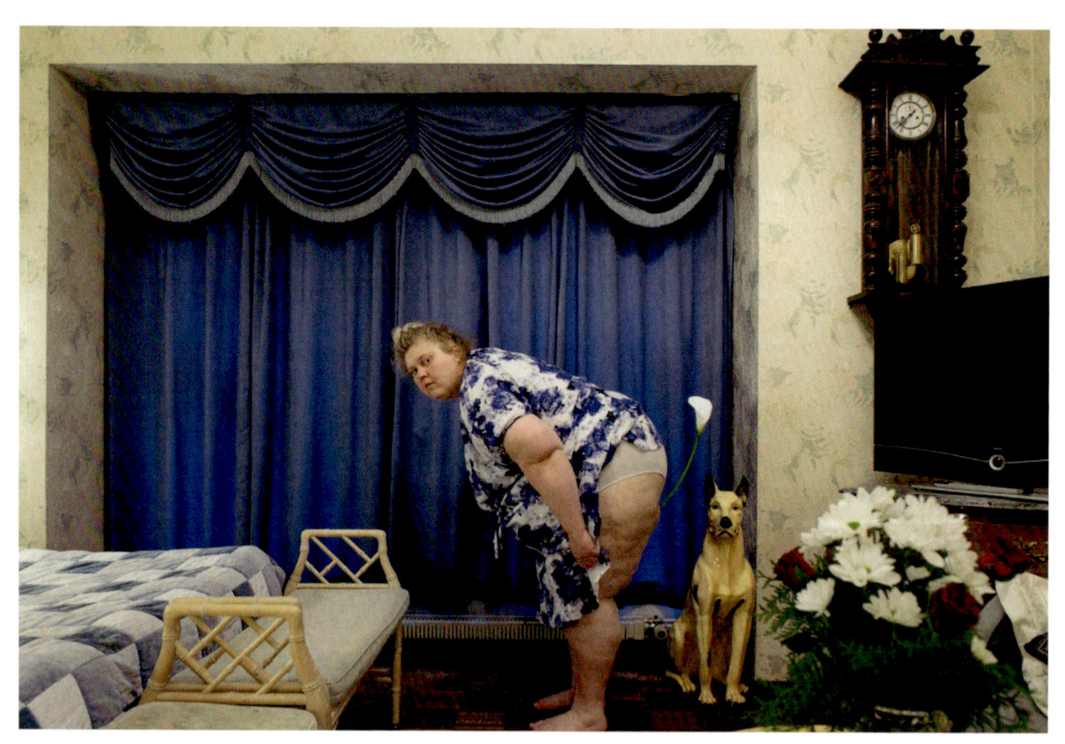

Pidät muusasi kylmänä.
Säilyryys on niin parempi.

Keep your muse cold.
Then they will last longer.

Kieli turvoksissa mietit, että minusta meni maku.

you with your
swollen tongue
wondered why I
had lost taste.

Kaunis tuhmuus
istuu sinuun.
On hartioistakin
sopiva.

Beautiful naughtiness
fits you.
It sits well on your
shoulders, too.

Säännöllinen rakkautemme. Happy Hour.

Our regular
love.
Happy Hour.

Halaan ympärilläsi
olevaa ilmaa.
Otan syliin.
Tehden siitä
hattaraa.

I hug the air around you.
I take you in my arms.
Turning it to candy floss.

Unohda muuttoilmoitus.
Jäisit minuun.

Forget that change
of address.
You'll stay in me.

Virikkeet vähissä.
Rauta kylmänä.
Matto vetää
suoruuttaan lattialla.
Puhun sille
muistellen sinua.

Incitements running low.
The iron is cold.
The rug straightens
out on the floor.
I talk to it with
you in mind.

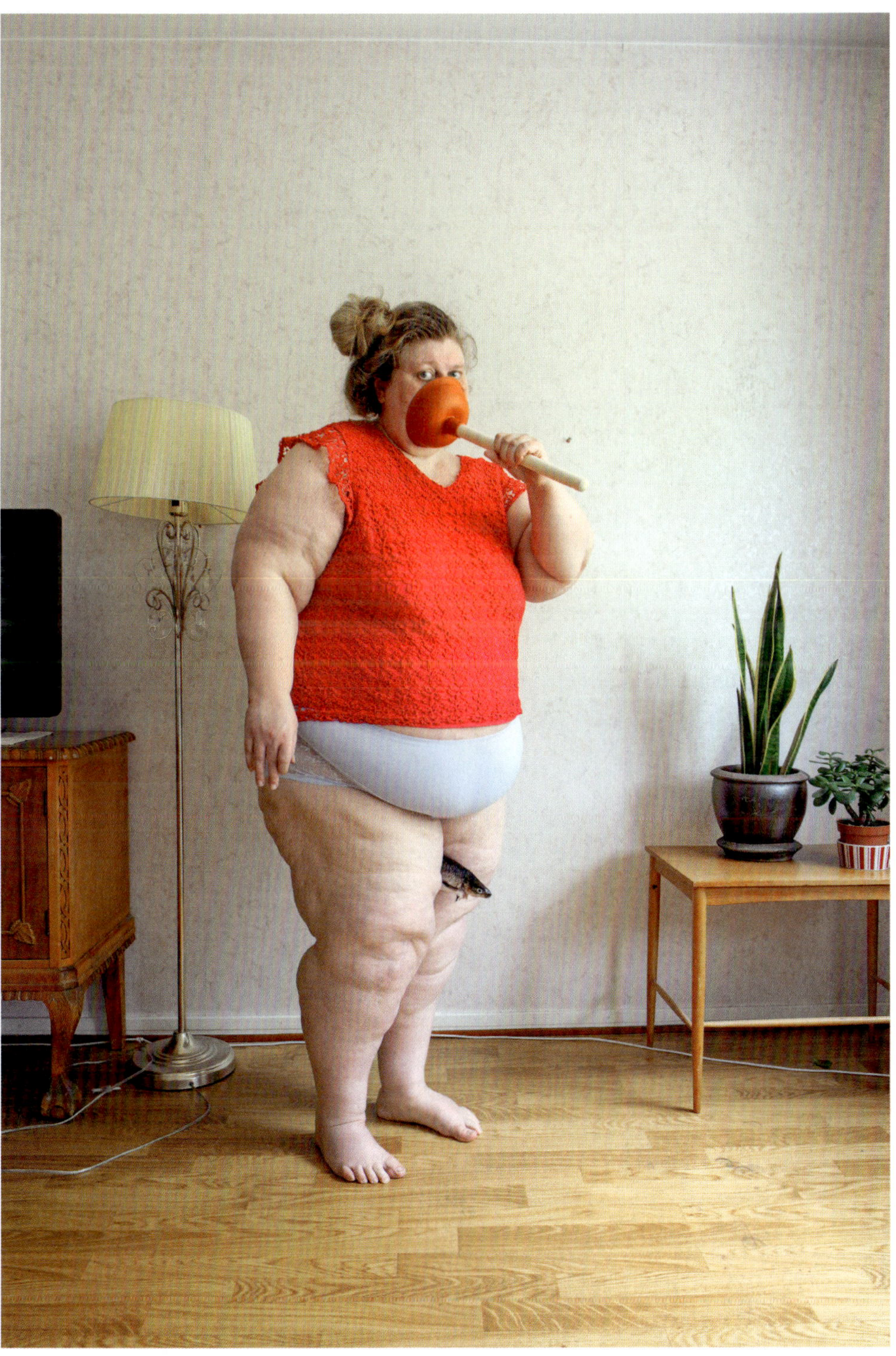

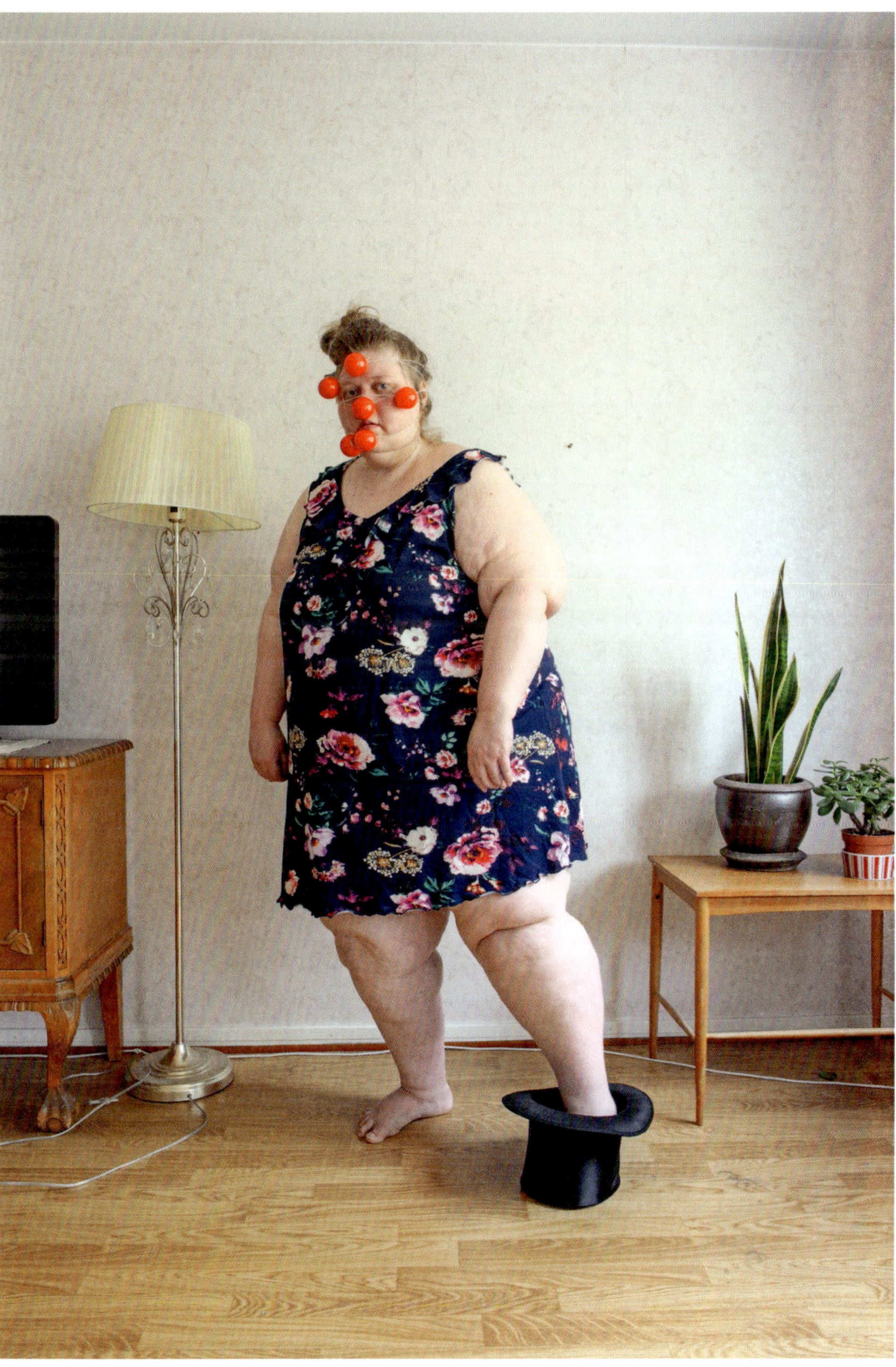

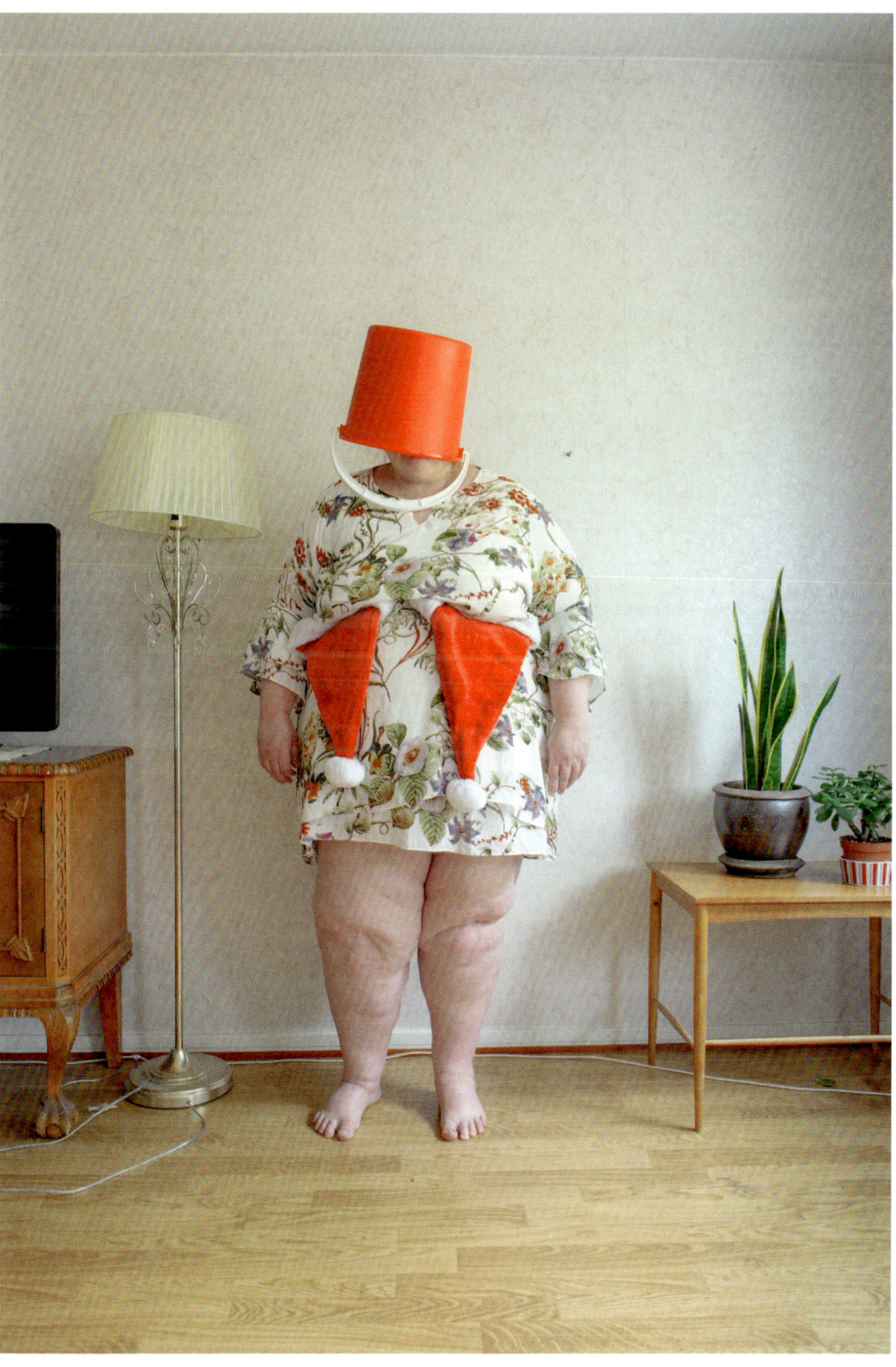

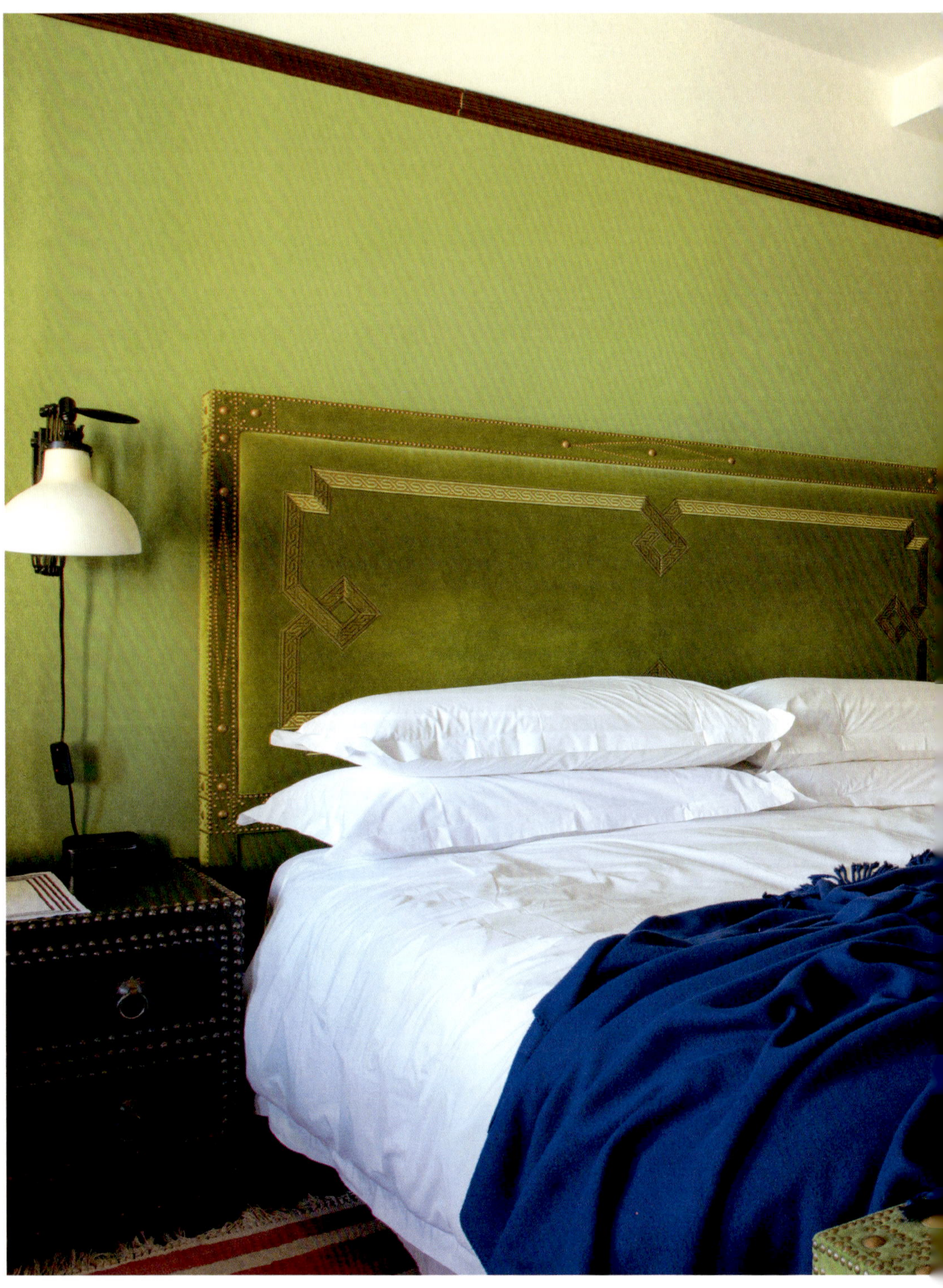

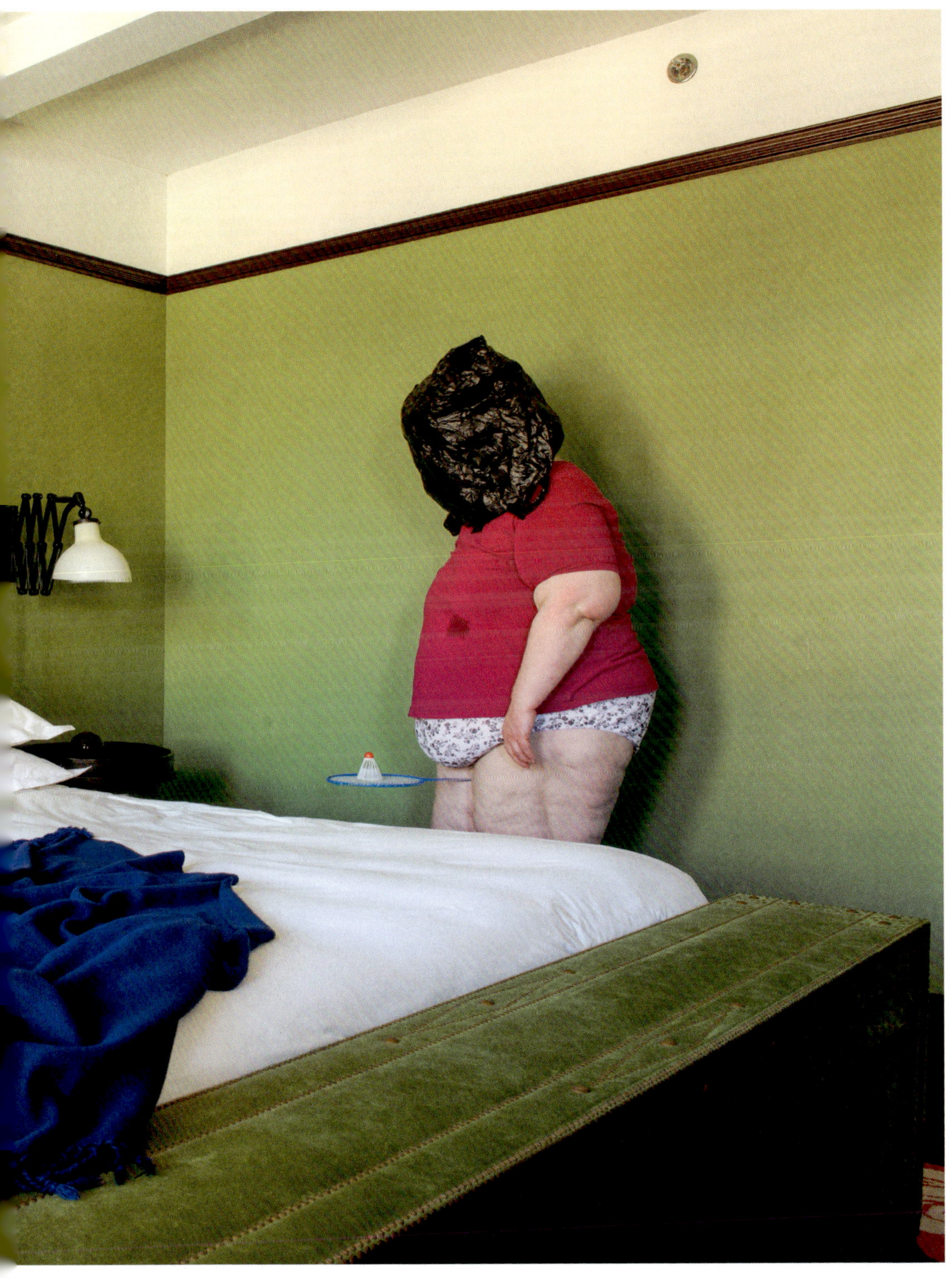

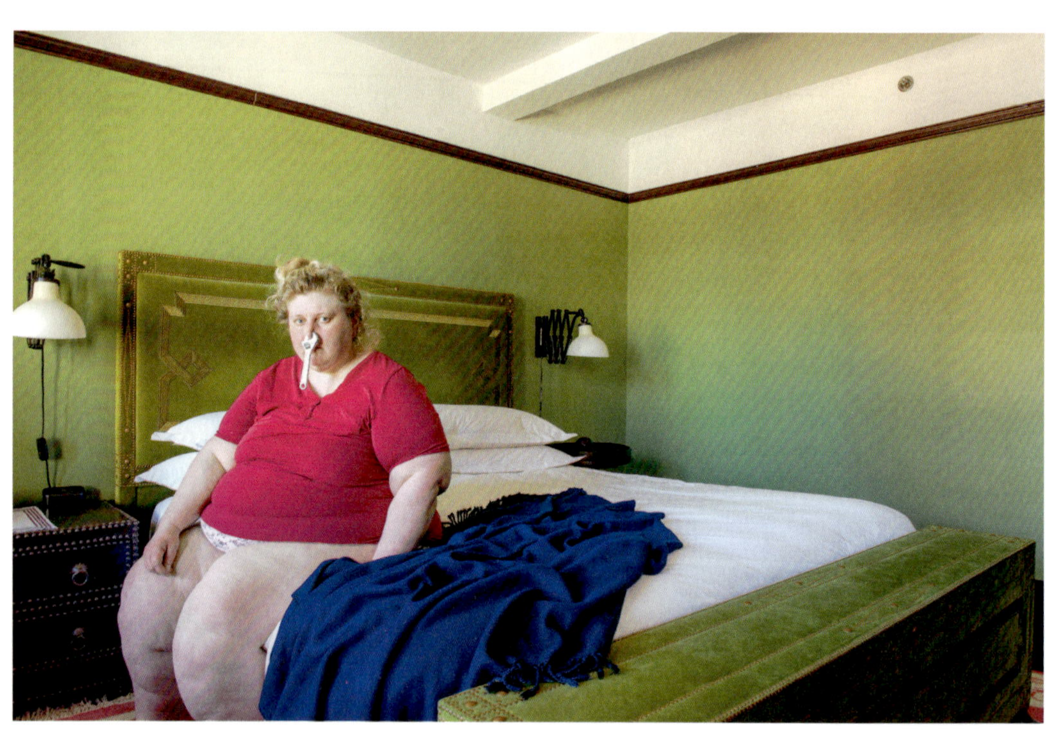

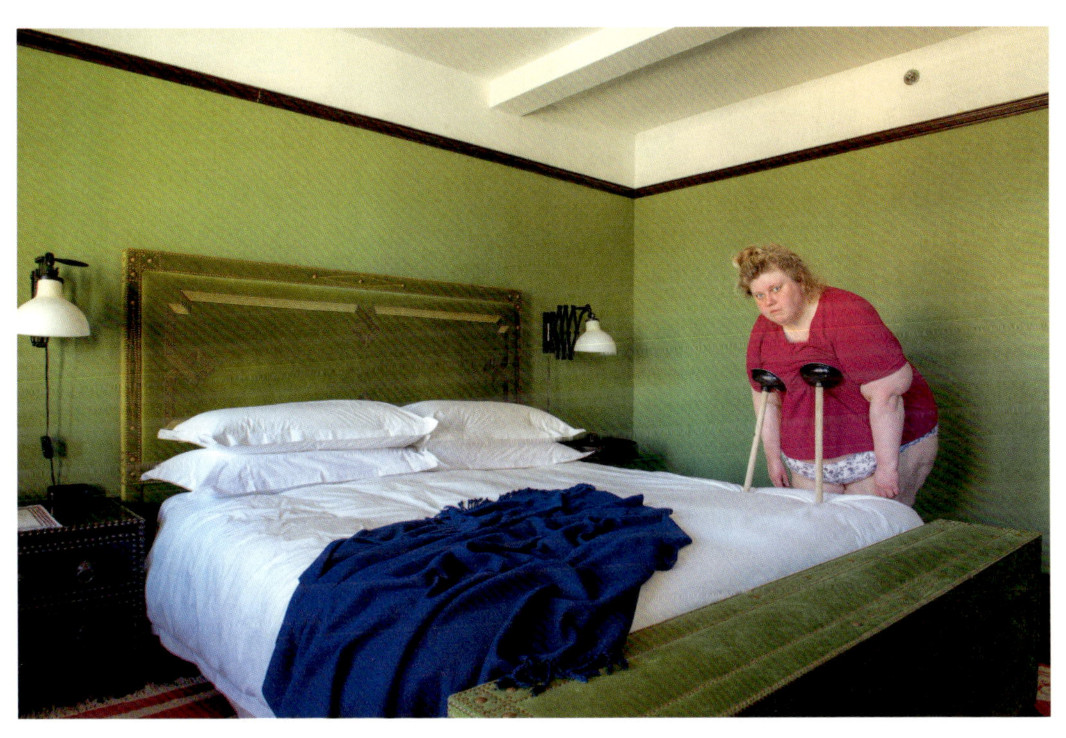

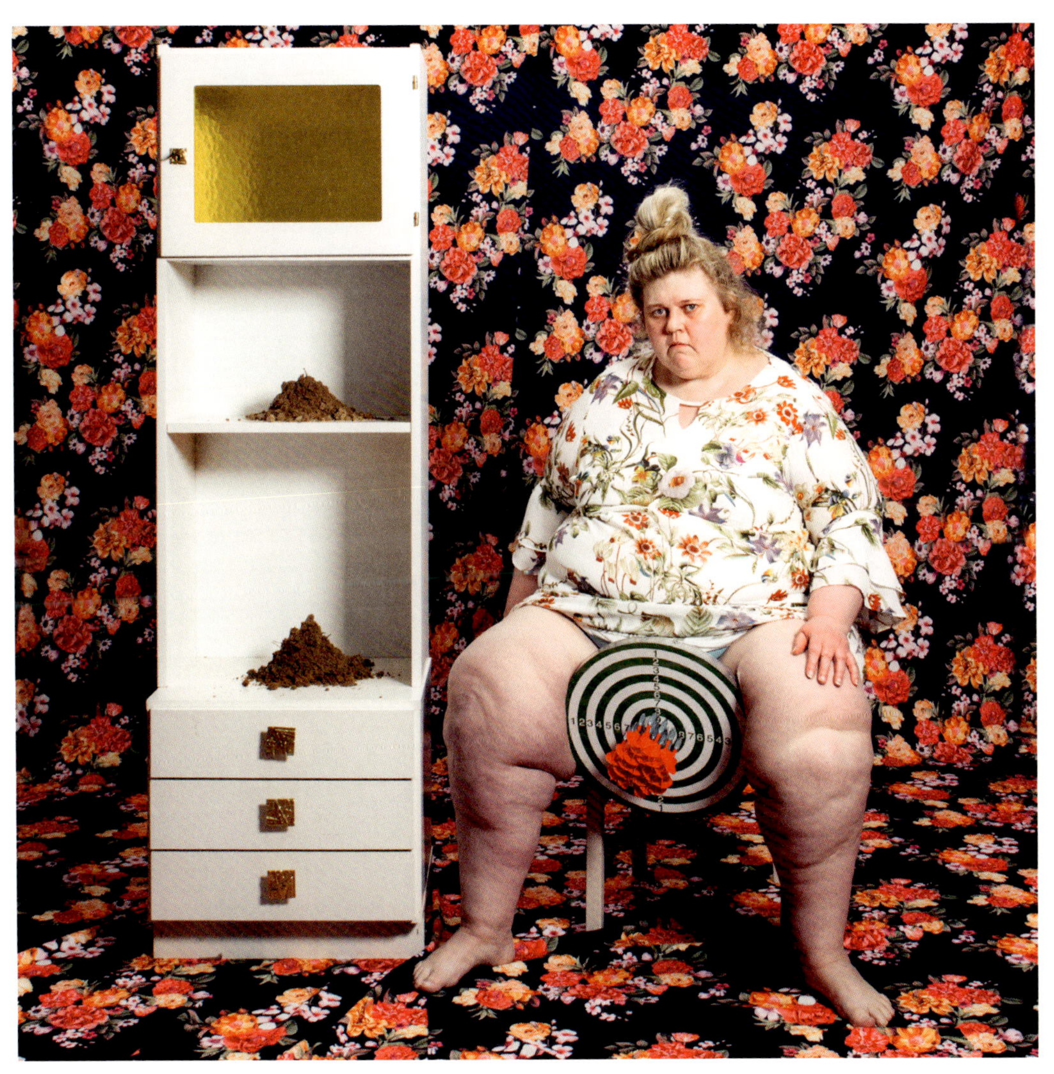

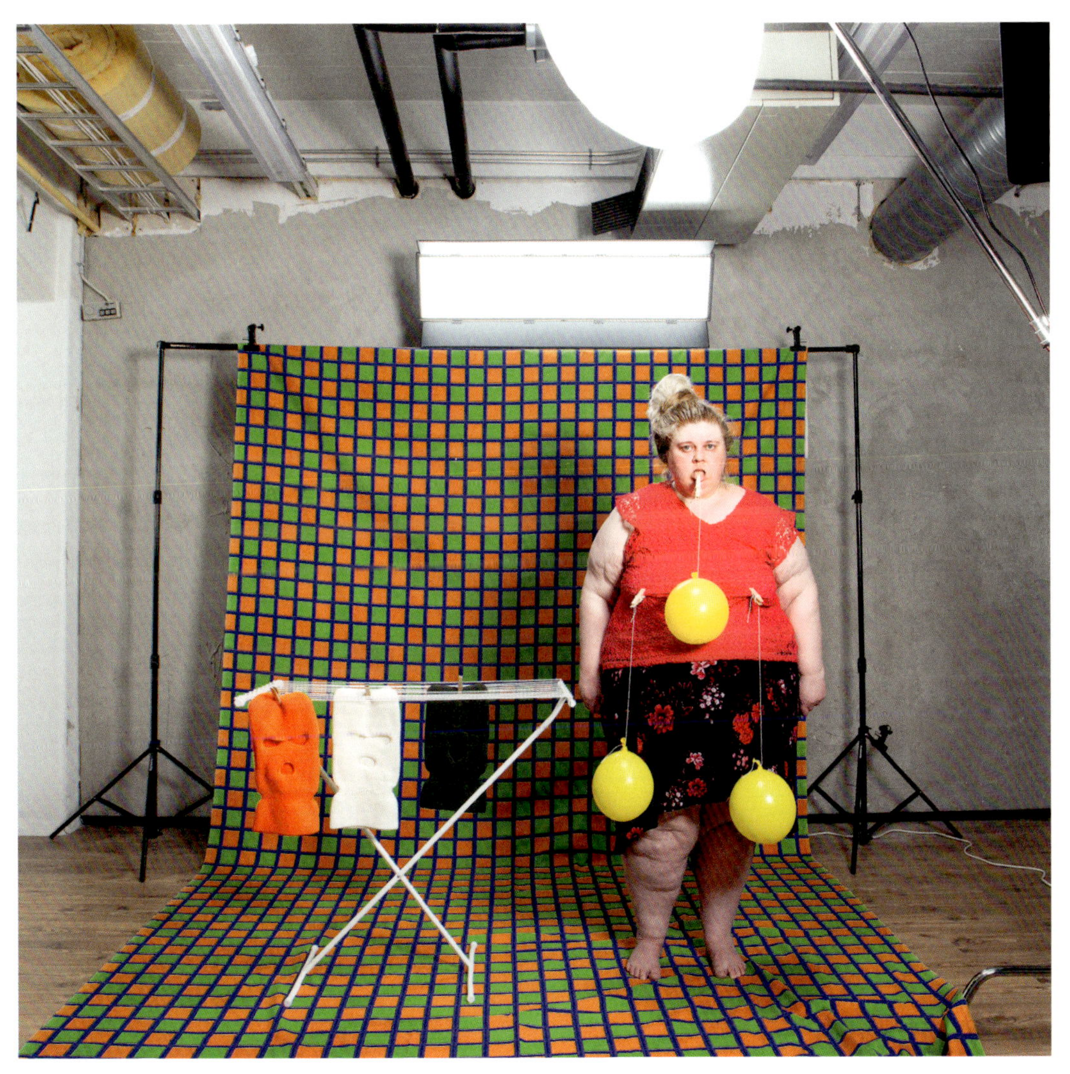

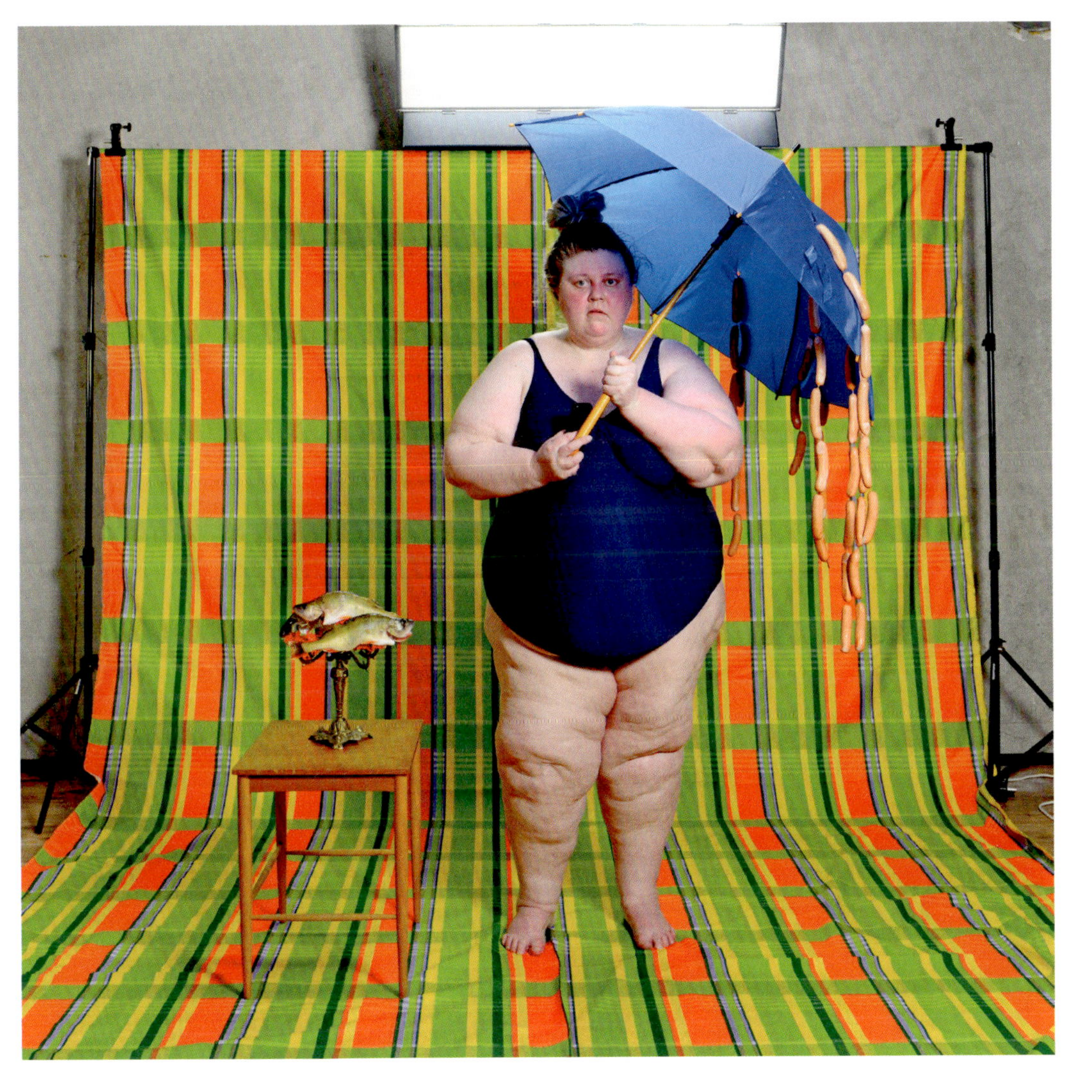

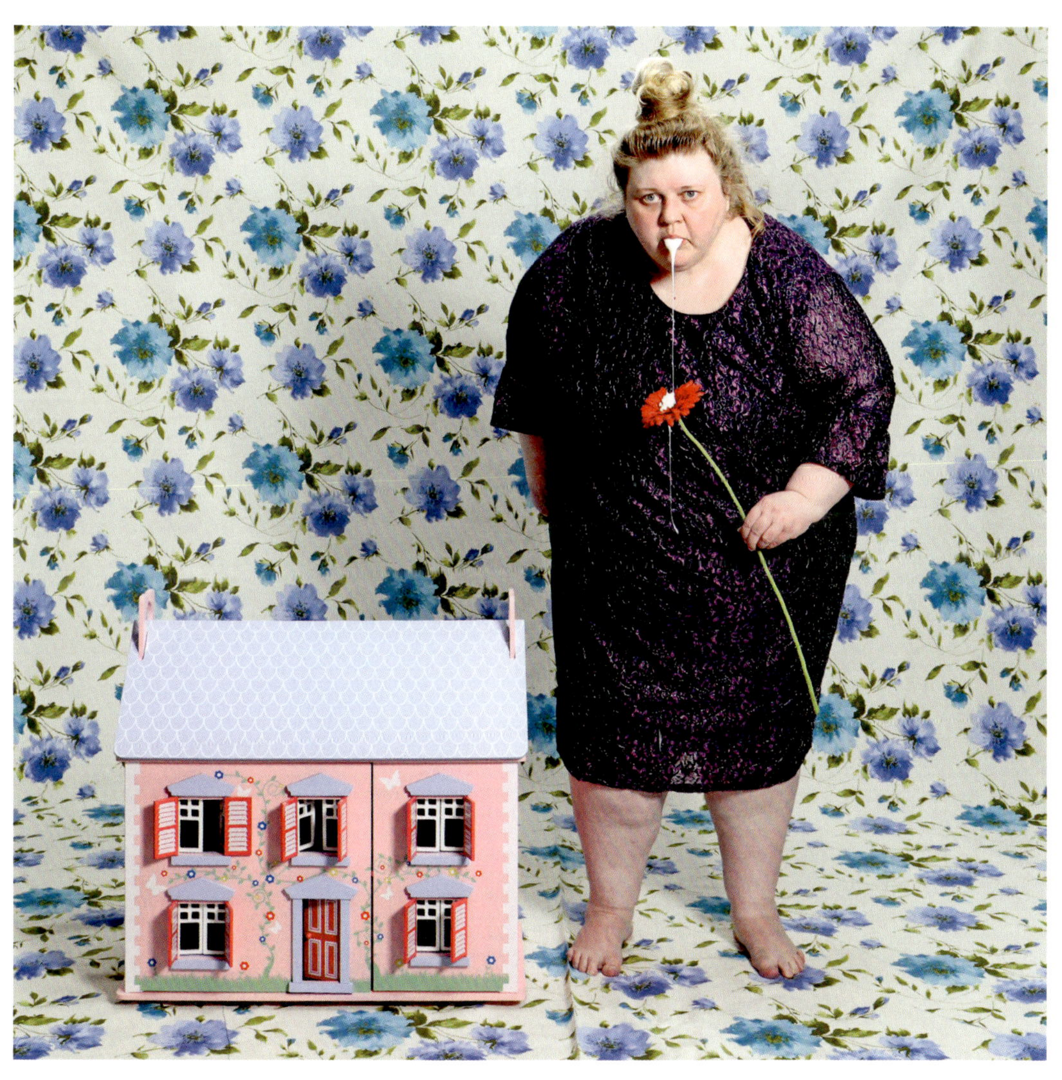

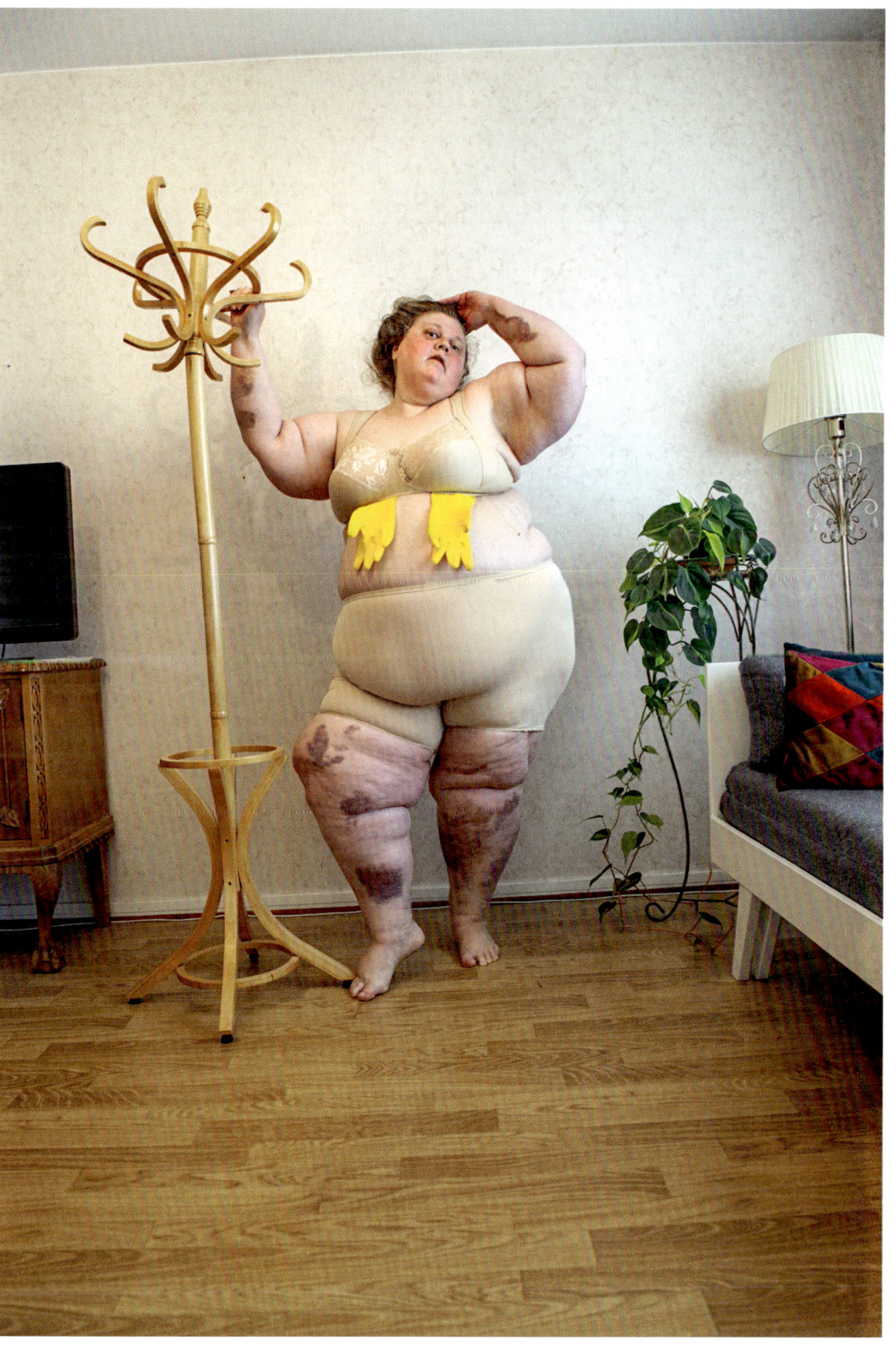

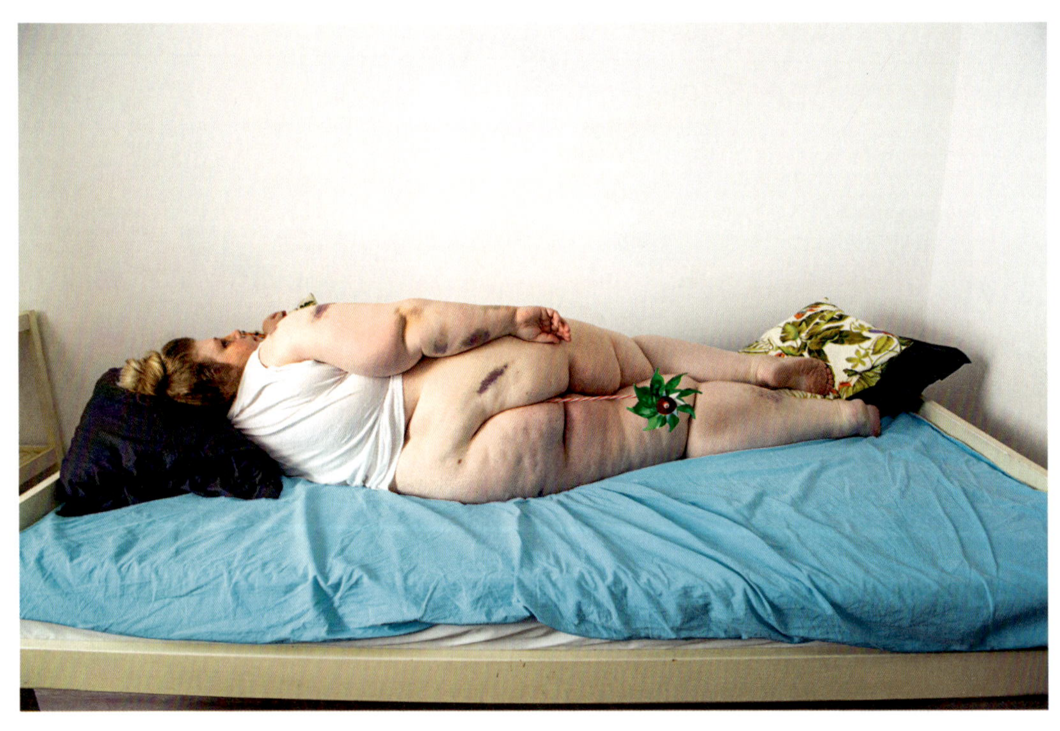

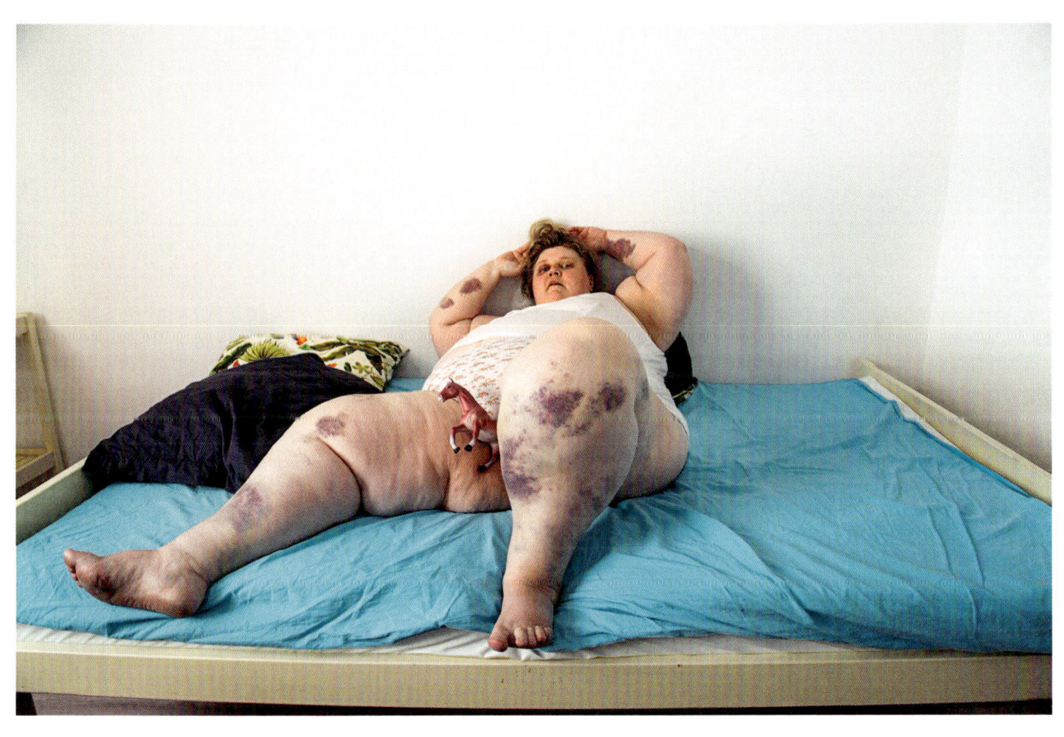

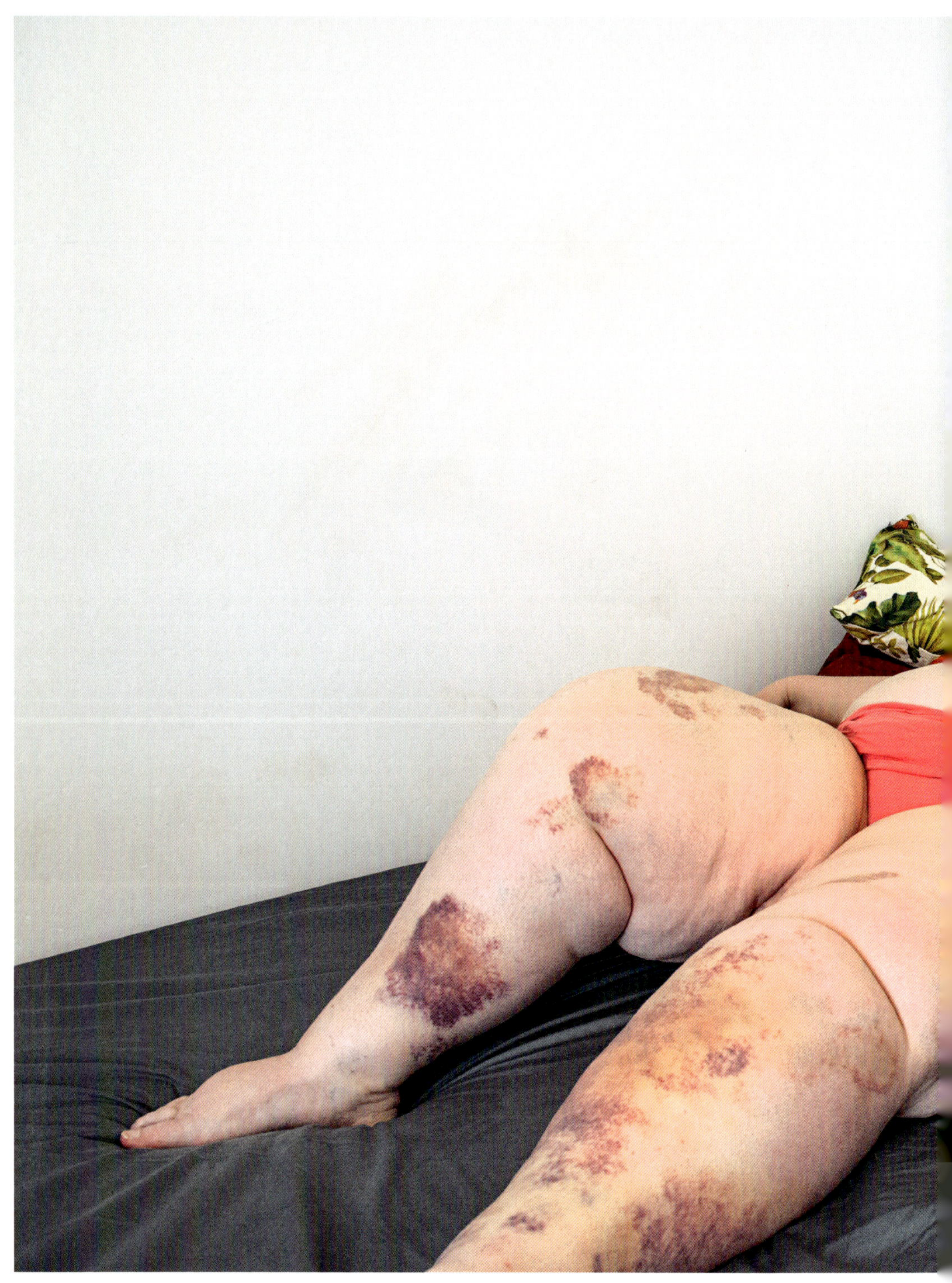

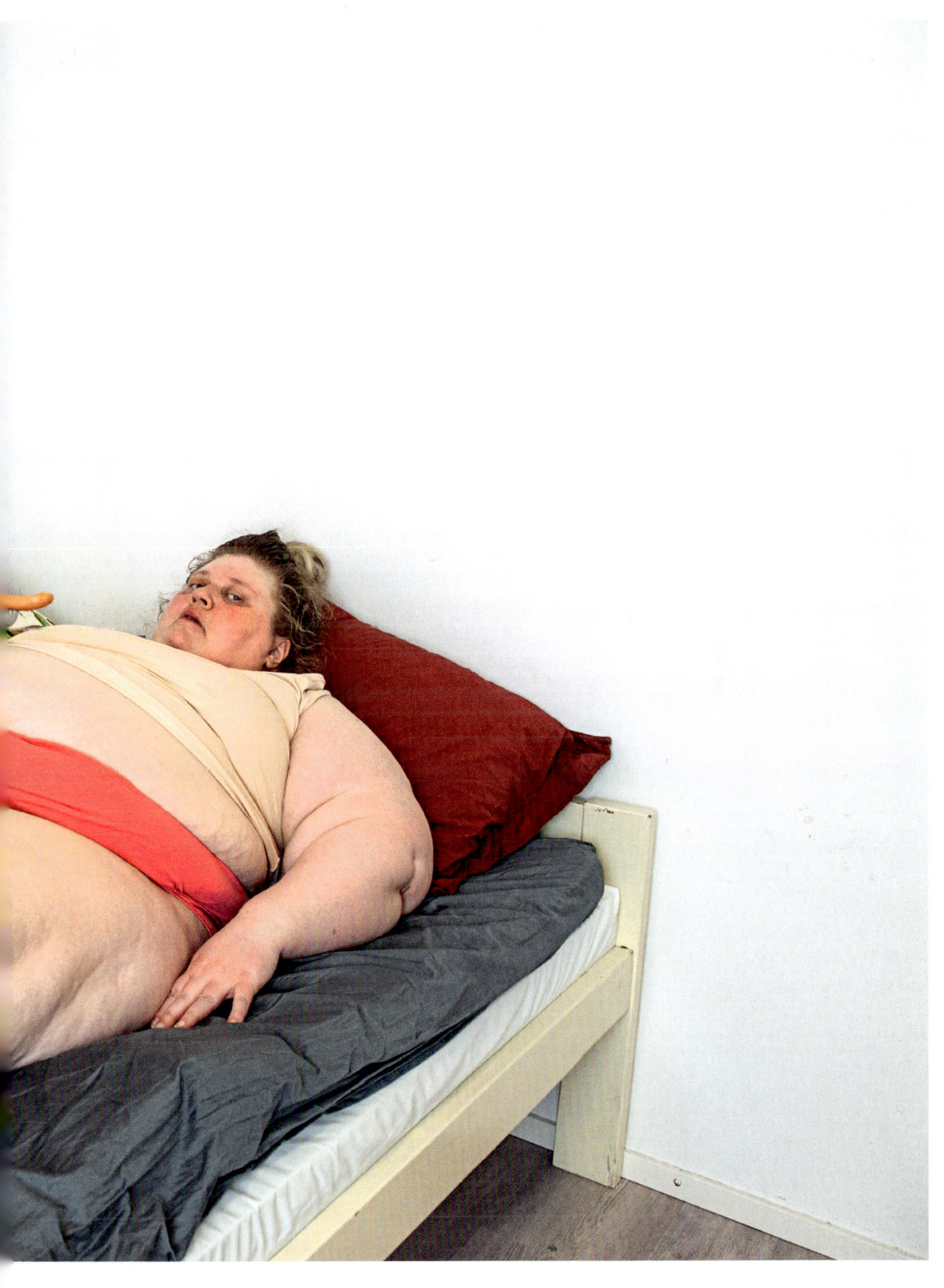

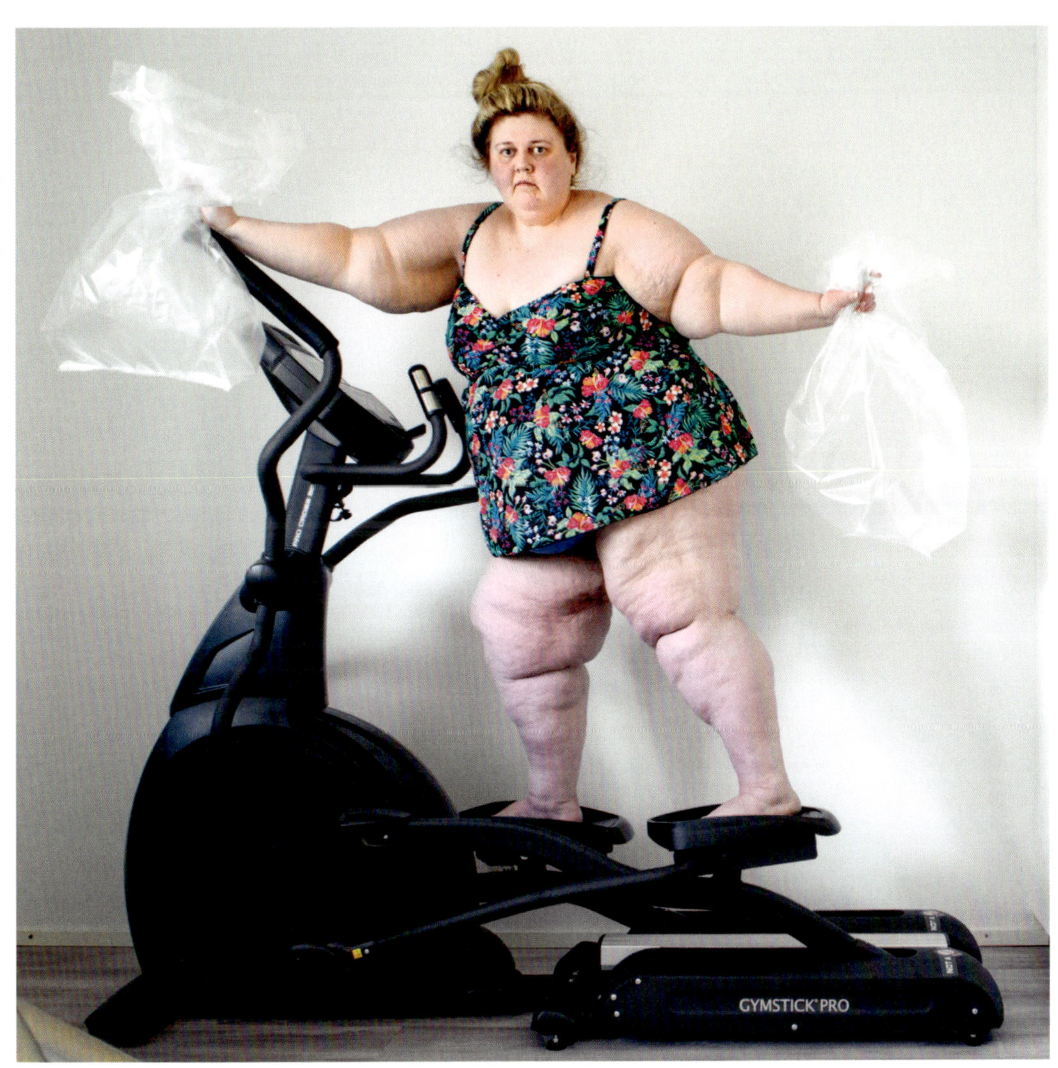
GYMSTICK PRO

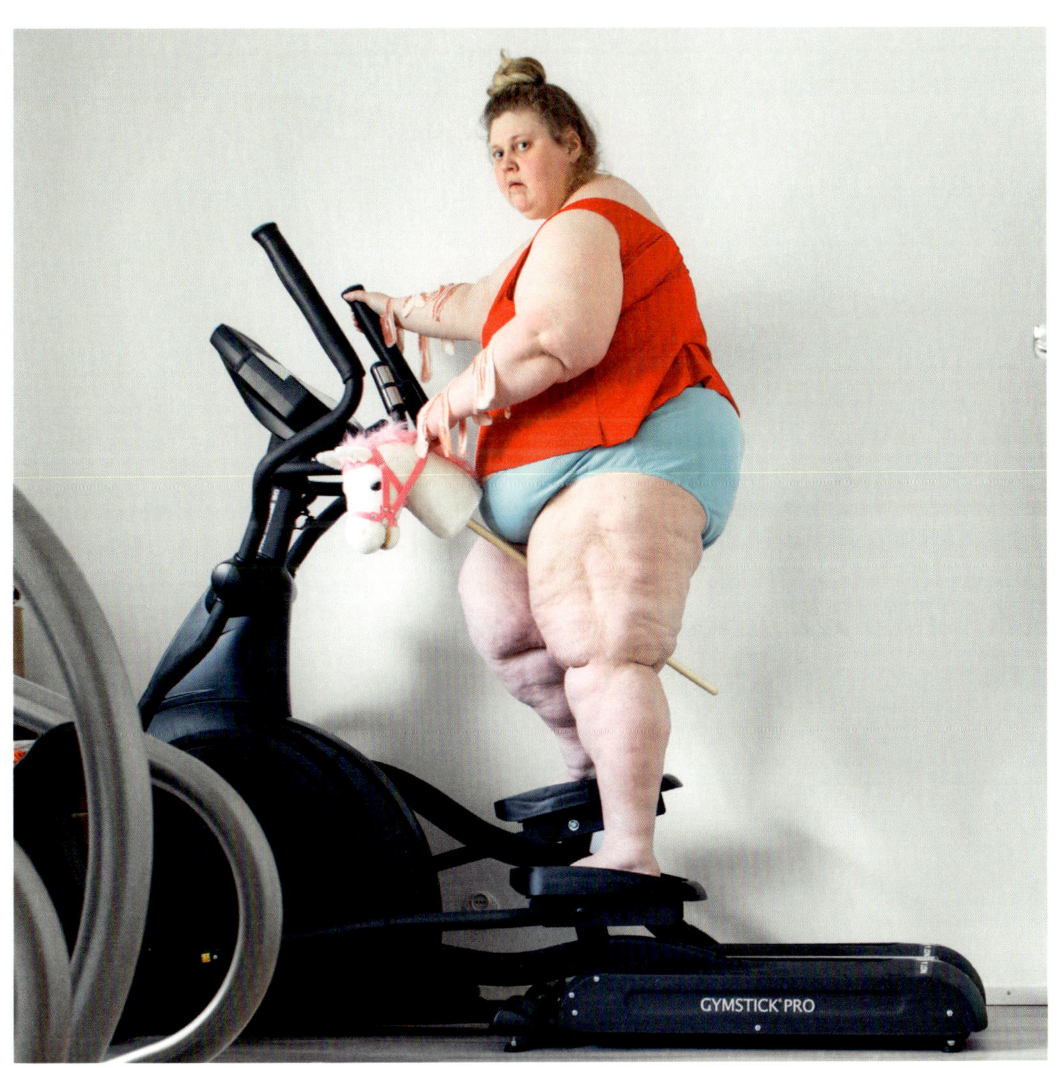

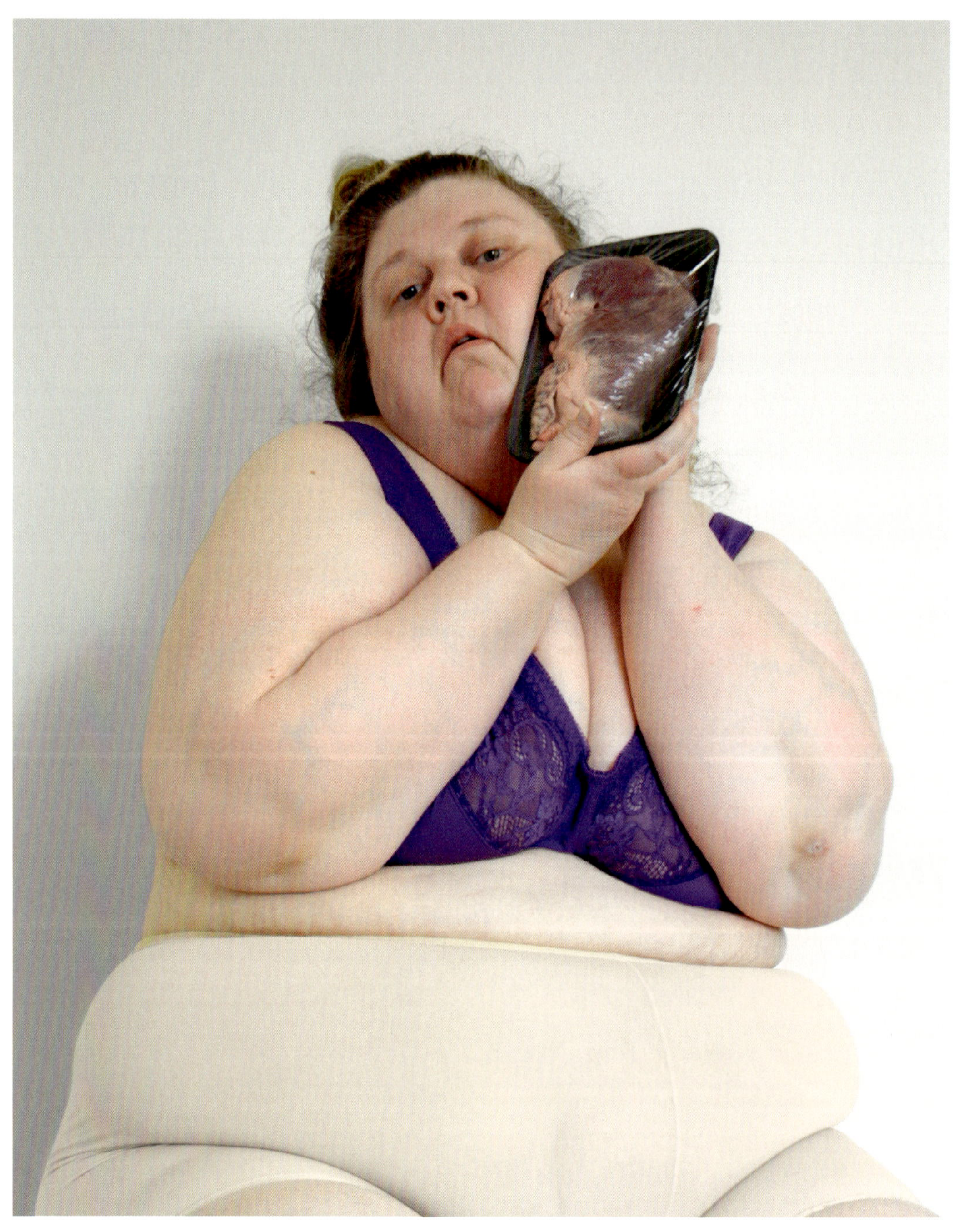

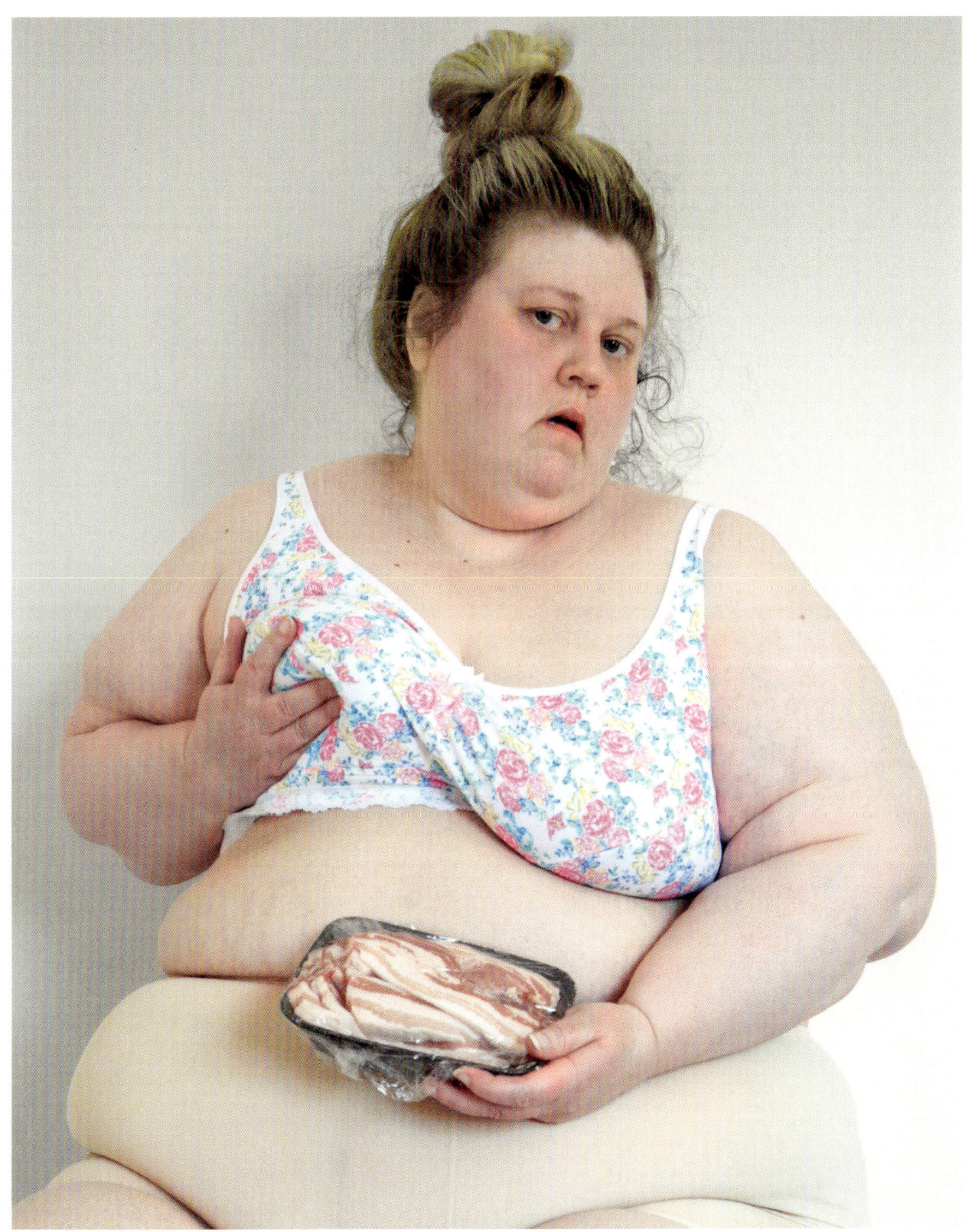

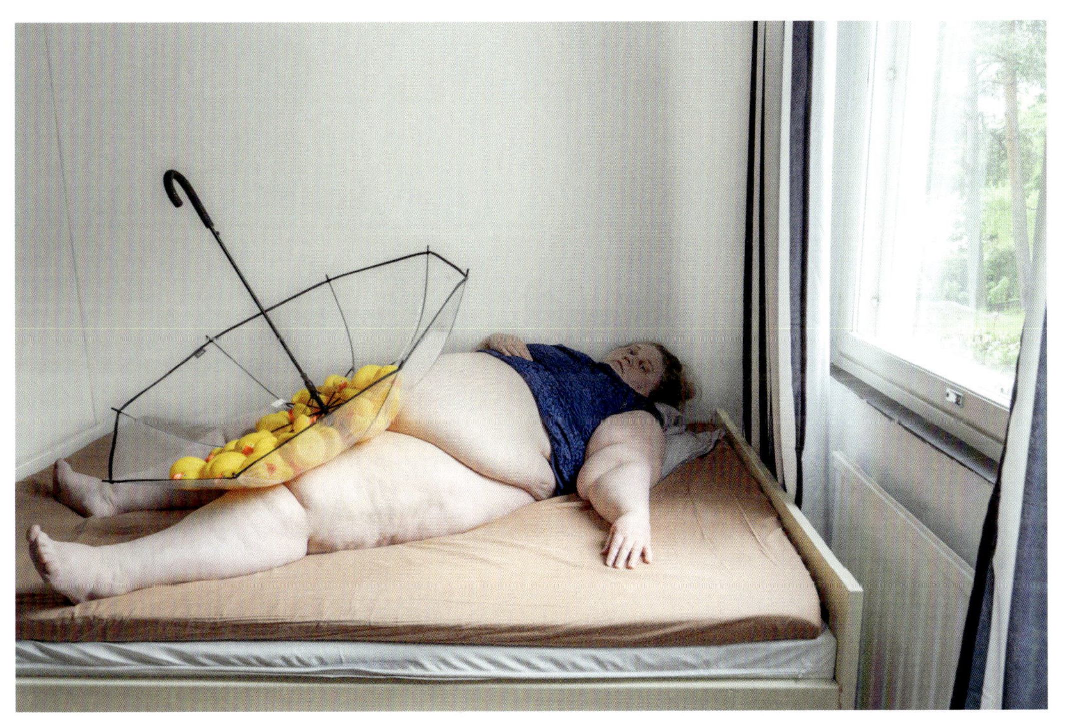

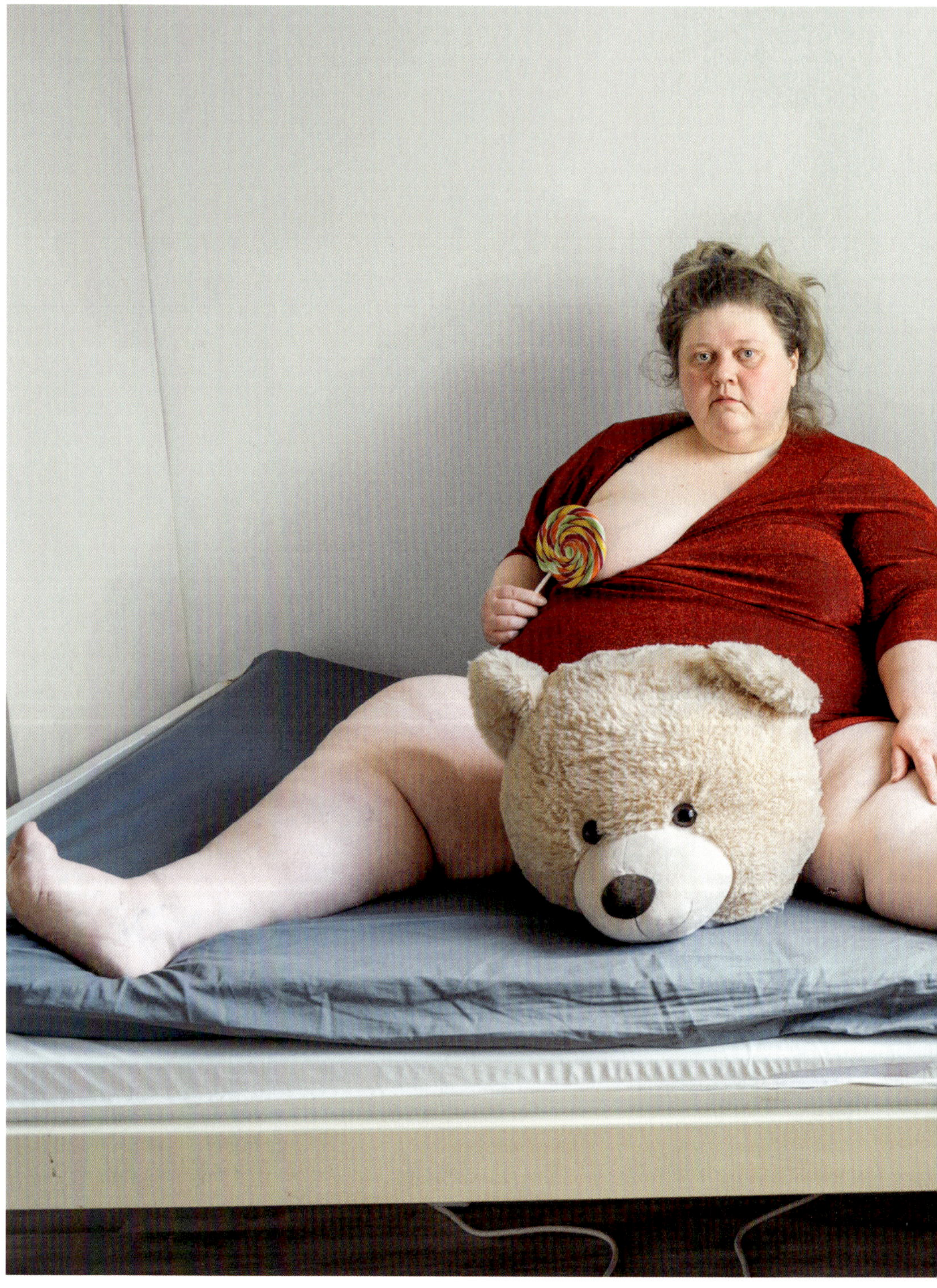

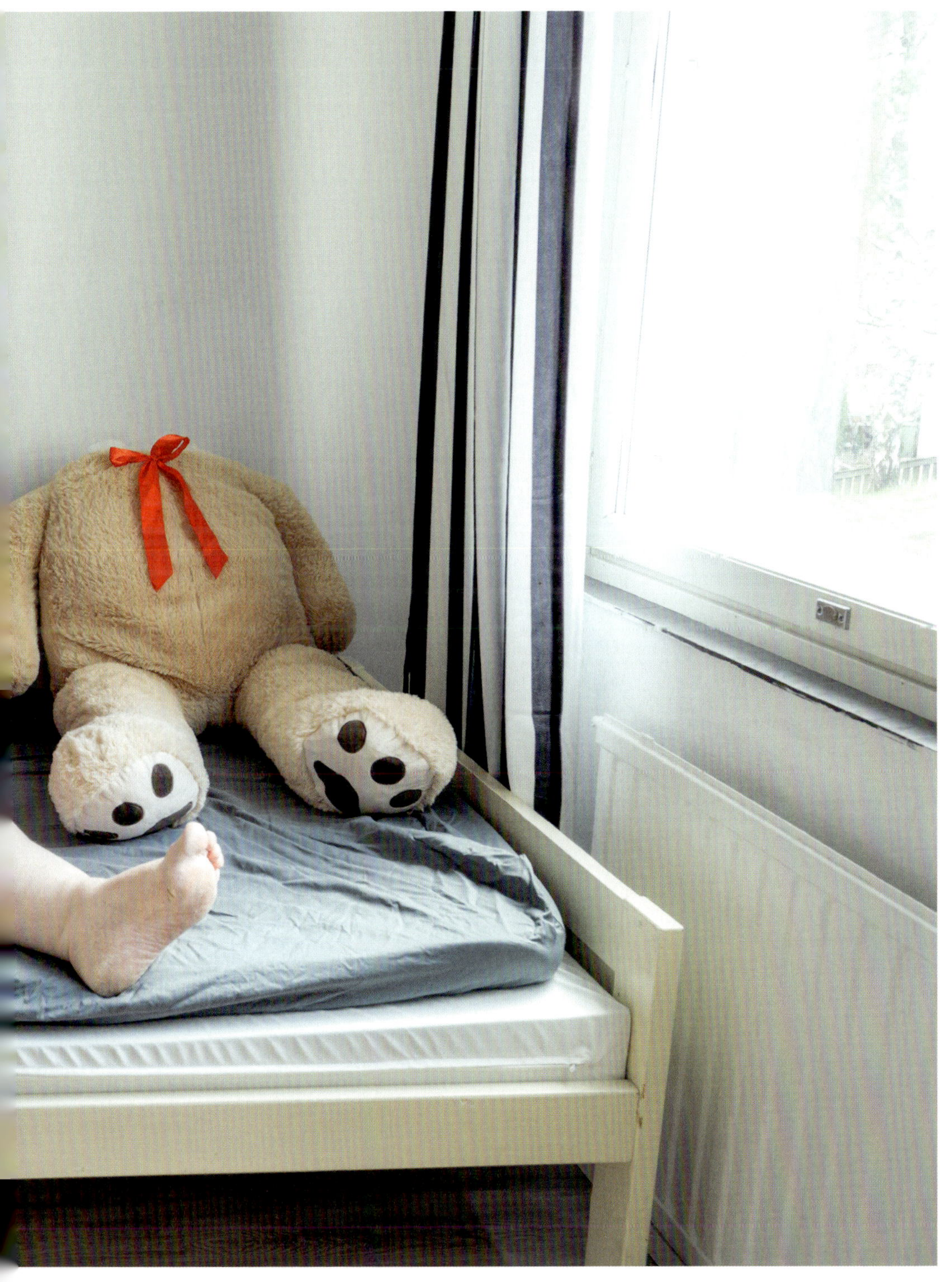

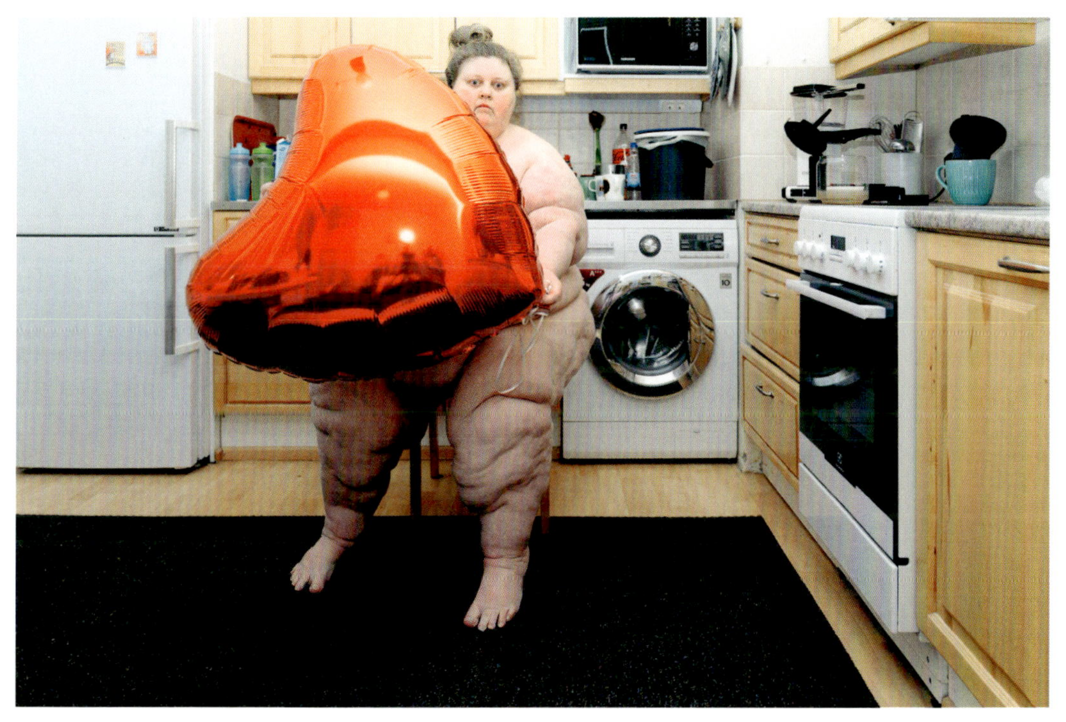

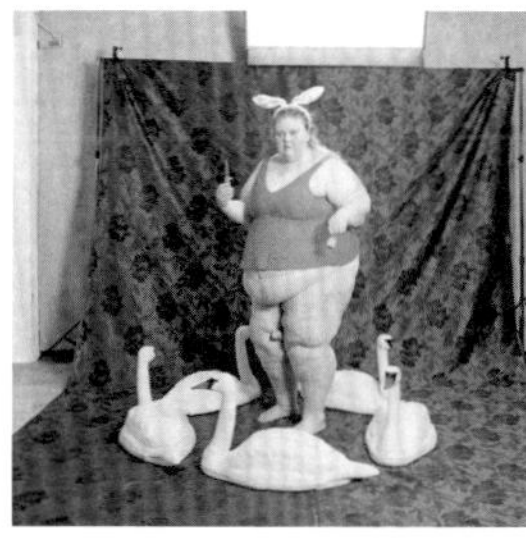

p. 1
Mad Bunny, 2019
Chromogenic print
23 ⅝ x 23 ⅝" (60 x 60 cm)
Courtesy the artist
and Makasiini Contemporary

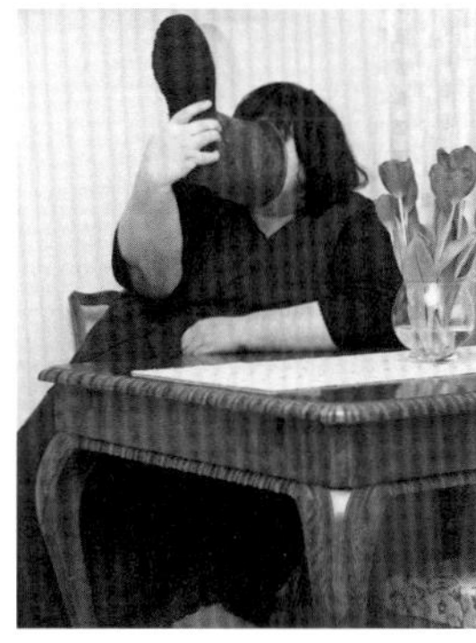

p. 21
Revolution, 2008
Chromogenic print
15 ¾ x 11 ¾" (40 x 29.8 cm)

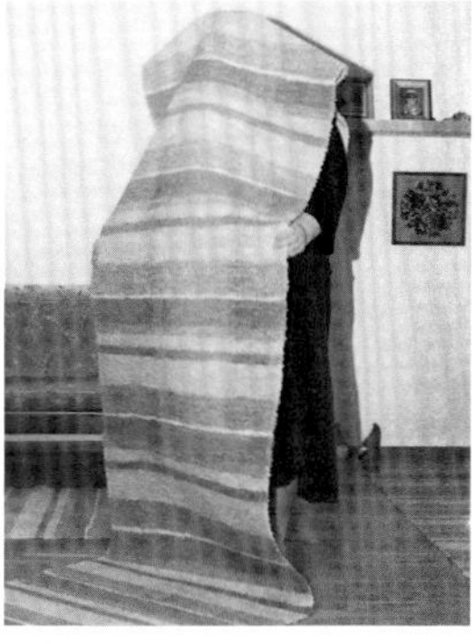

p. 23
Large-scale cleaning, 2008
Chromogenic print
15 ¾ x 11 ¾" (40 x 29.8 cm)

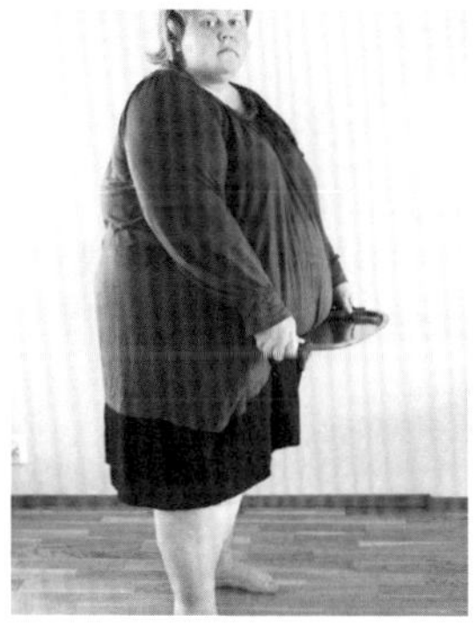

p. 25
Self-service, 2009*
Chromogenic print
12 ⅜ x 10 ⅝" (31.5 x 27 cm)

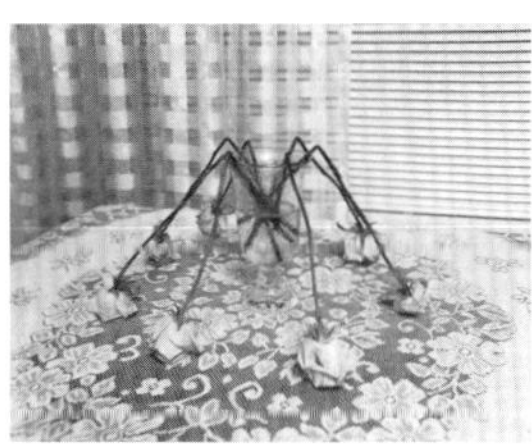

p. 27
Spider, 2009*
Chromogenic print
Dimensions variable

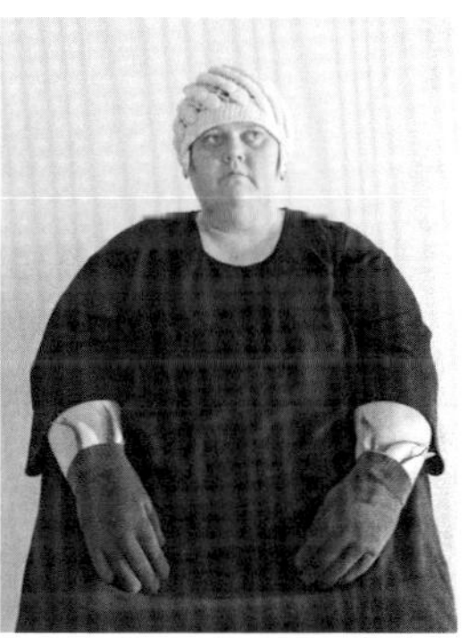

p. 29
Woman, 2010
Chromogenic print
33 ½ x 25 ⅛" (85.1 x 63.8 cm)

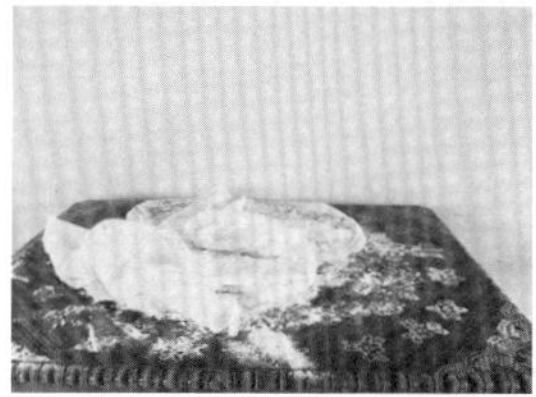

p. 30
Floury cloth, 2010
Chromogenic print
11 ¾ x 15 ¾" (29.8 x 40 cm)

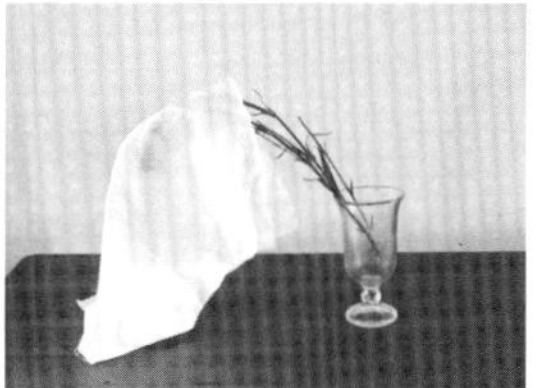

p. 33
When I touch the flowers,
2010
Chromogenic print
11 ¾ x 15 ¾" (29.8 x 40 cm)

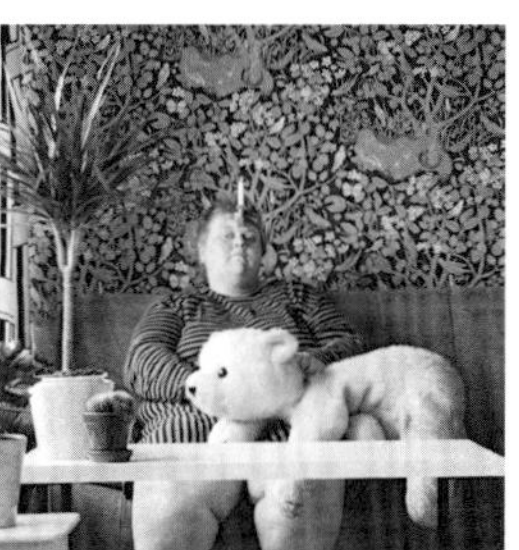

p. 35
Lucia, 2010
Chromogenic print
16 x 15 ¾" (40.6 x 40 cm)
(framed)
Collection Glori Cohen

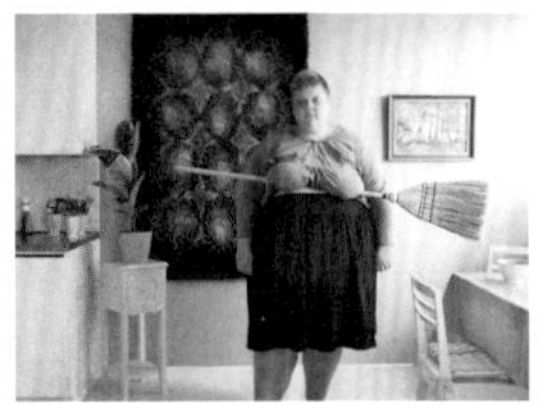

p. 37
Broom, 2010
Chromogenic print
12 ½ x 16″ (31.8 x 40.6 cm)
(framed)
Collection Glori Cohen

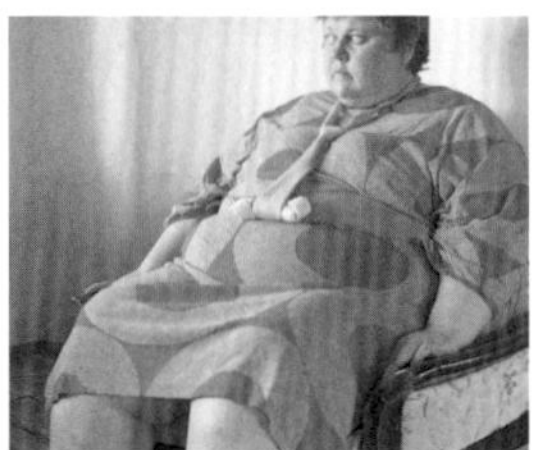

p. 39
Puruluu (Chewing bone), 2010
Chromogenic print
11 ⅜ x 13 ½″ (29 x 34.3 cm)

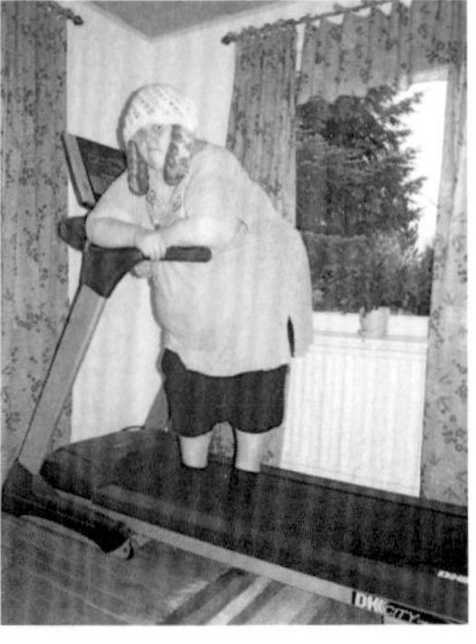

p. 41
Training, 2010
Chromogenic print
28 x 21″ (71.1 x 53.3 cm)

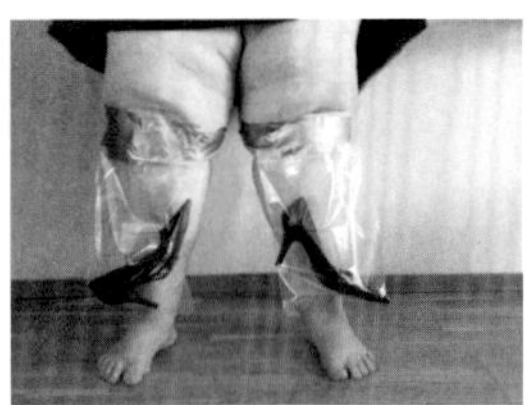

p. 43
Bad legs, 2010
Chromogenic print
11 ¾ x 15 ¾″ (29.8 x 40 cm)

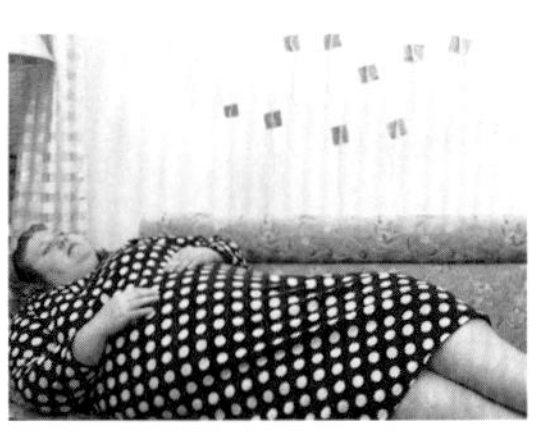

p. 44
Al dente, 2010*
Chromogenic print
10 ⅝ x 12 ⅜″ (27 x 31.5 cm)

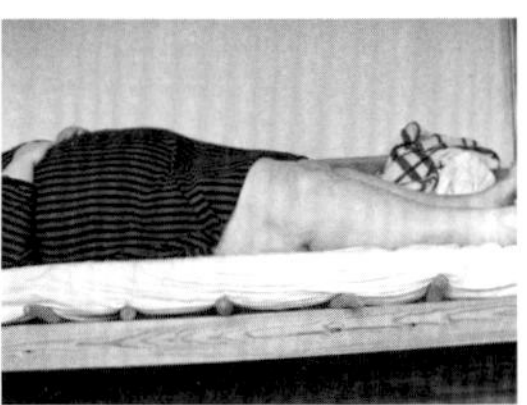

p. 46
Carrots, 2010*
Chromogenic print
10 ⅝ x 12 ⅜″ (27 x 31.5 cm)

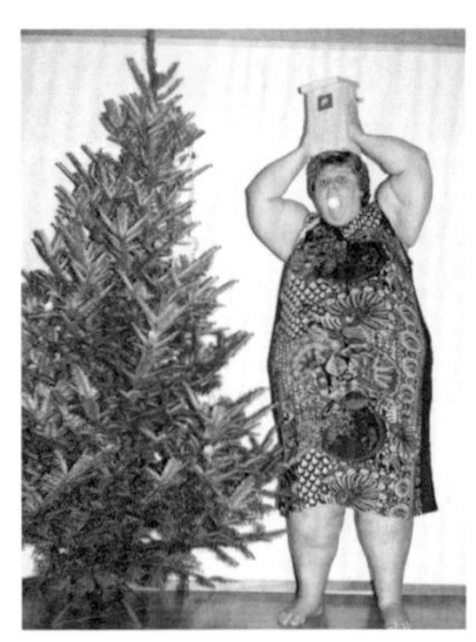

p. 49
Spruce, 2010
Chromogenic print
13 x 9 ¾″ (33 x 24.8 cm)

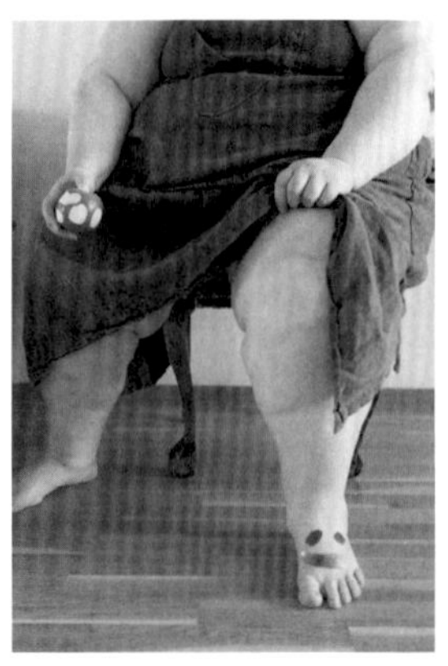

p. 51
Happy meal, 2011
Chromogenic print
15 ¾ x 10 ½″ (40 x 26.7 cm)

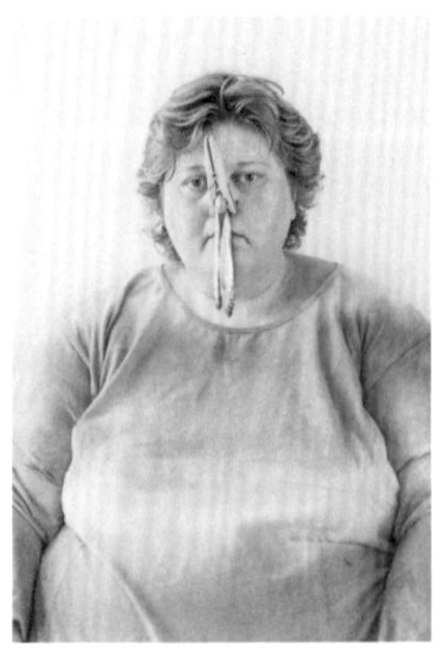

p. 53
Hajuton ja mauton (Odorless and tasteless), 2011
Chromogenic print
15 ¾ x 10 ½″ (40 x 26.7 cm)

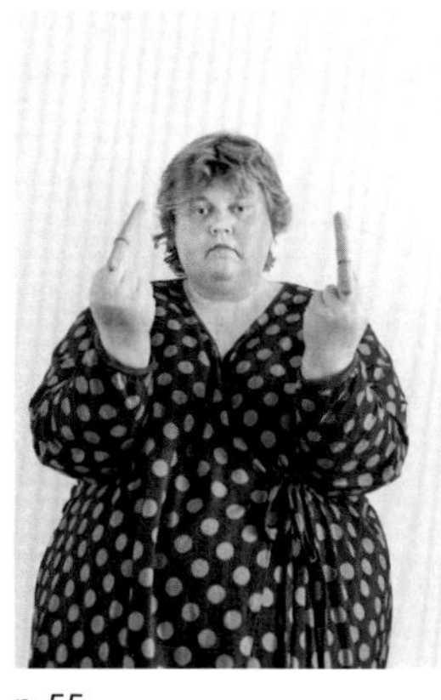

p. 55
Haista nakki (Smell the sausage), 2011
Chromogenic print
15 ³/₄ x 10 ½" (40 x 26.7 cm)

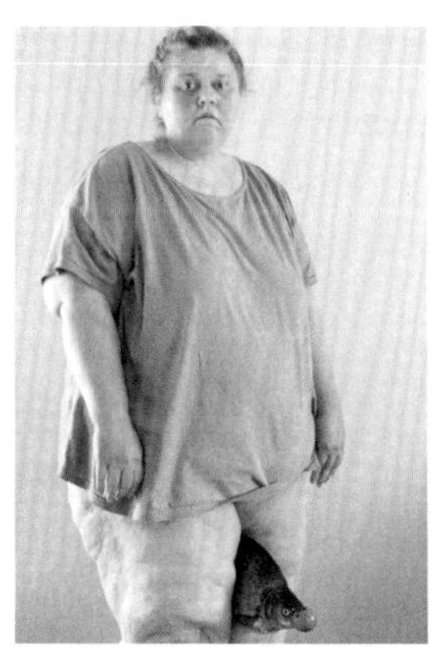

p. 61
Valta (Power), 2014
Chromogenic print
30 x 20" (76.2 x 50.8 cm)

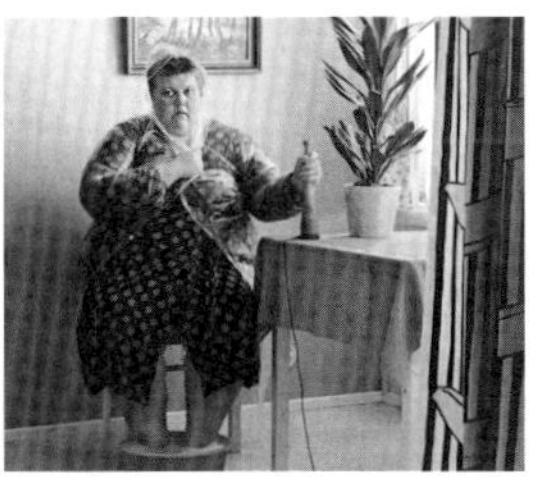

p. 57
*Perinnepirkot huomio 1
(Attention, traditional
women 1)*, 2012
Chromogenic print
11 ⁷/₈ x 13 ½" (30.1 x 34.3 cm)

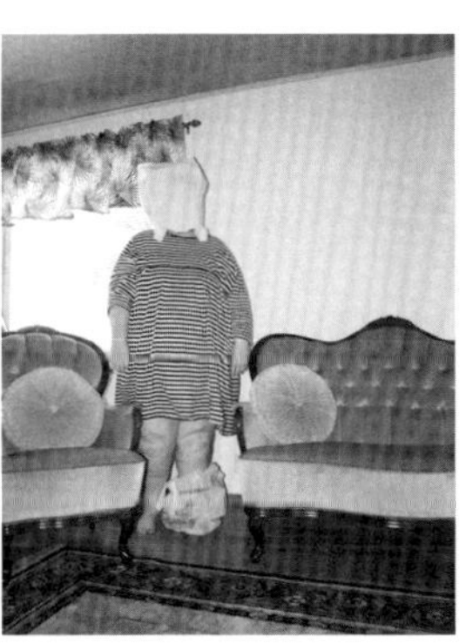

p. 63
Afternoon on the divan 1, 2016
Chromogenic print
35 x 26 ¼" (88.9 x 66.7 cm)

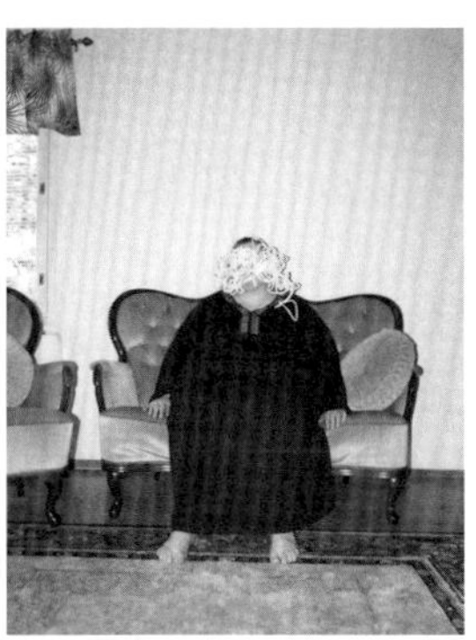

p. 67
Afternoon on the divan 3,
2016
Chromogenic print
35 x 26 ¼" (88.9 x 66.7 cm)

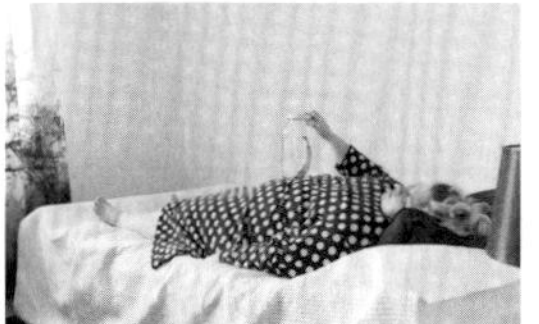

p. 58
Functional communication,
2012
Chromogenic print
20 x 30" (50.8 x 76.2 cm)

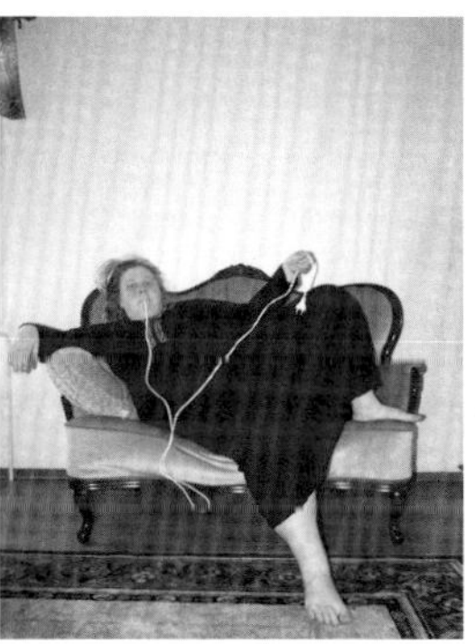

p. 65
Afternoon on the divan 2,
2016
Chromogenic print
35 x 26 ¼" (88.9 x 66.7 cm)

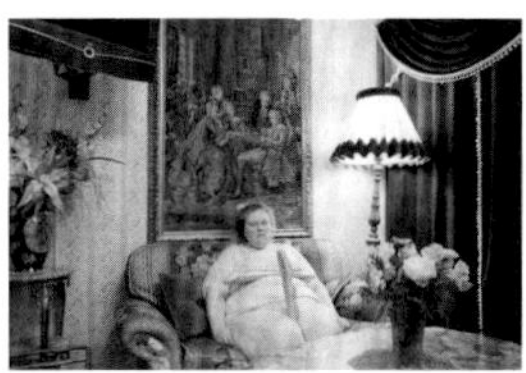

p. 69
Patongit (French loafs), 2017
Chromogenic print
10 ⁷/₁₆ x 13 ¹¹/₁₆" (26.5 x 34.7
cm) (framed)
Private collection

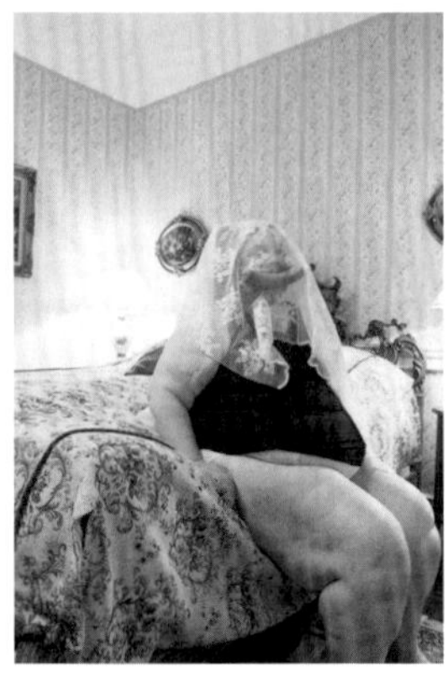

p. 71
Iloinen morsian (Happy bride),
2017
Chromogenic print
13 11/16 x 10 7/16"
(34.7 x 26.5 cm) (framed)
Collection Mark Miller,
New York

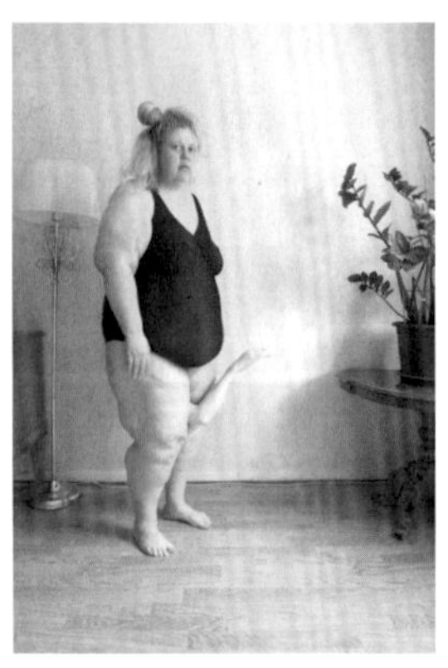

p. 76
Kättely (Handshake), 2017
Chromogenic print
13 11/16 x 10 7/16" (34.7 x 26.5
cm) (framed)
Collection Kevin Yao and
Judy Chen

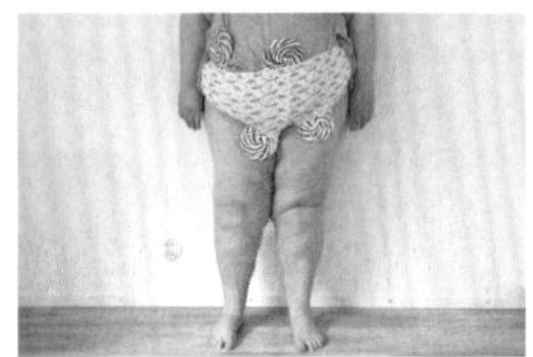

p. 80
Candy, 2017
Chromogenic print
6 11/16 x 9 13/16" (17 x 25 cm)

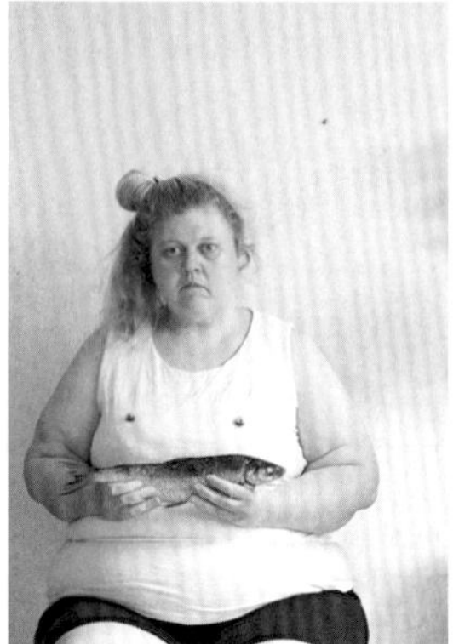

p. 73
Silmät (Eyes), 2017
Chromogenic print
9 13/16 x 6 11/16" (25 x 17 cm)

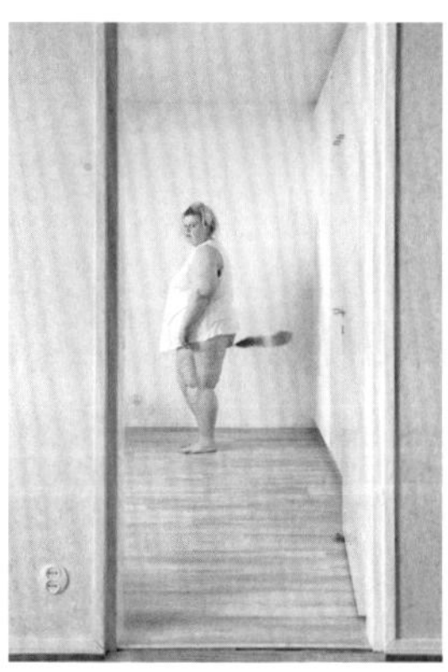

p. 77
*Siivouspalvelu (Housekeeping
service)*, 2017
Chromogenic print
13 11/16 x 10 7/16" (34.7 x 26.5
cm) (framed)
Collection Martin and
Rebecca Eisenberg

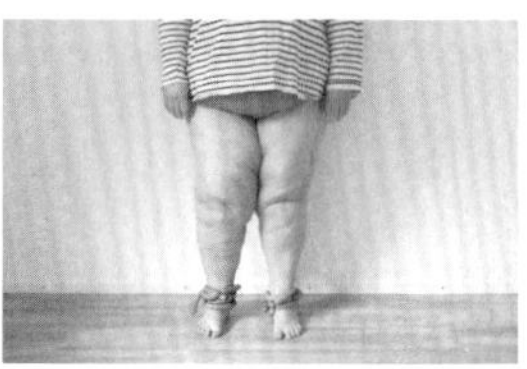

p. 81
Ankle weights, 2017
Chromogenic print
6 11/16 x 9 13/16" (17 x 25 cm)

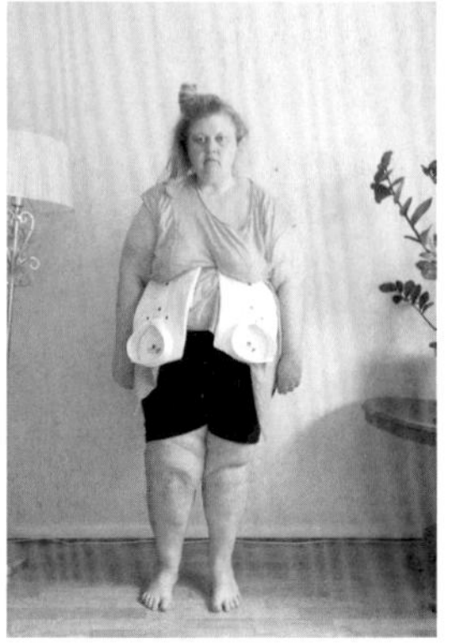

p. 75
Shirts, 2017
Chromogenic print
9 13/16 x 6 11/16" (25 x 17 cm)

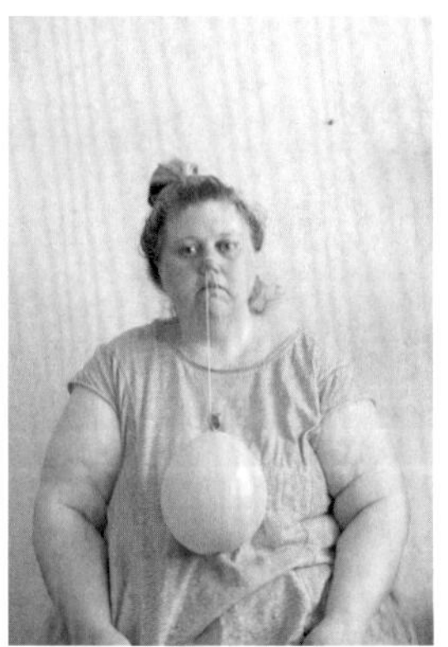

p. 79
Duo, 2017
Chromogenic print
9 13/16 x 6 11/16" (25 x 17 cm)

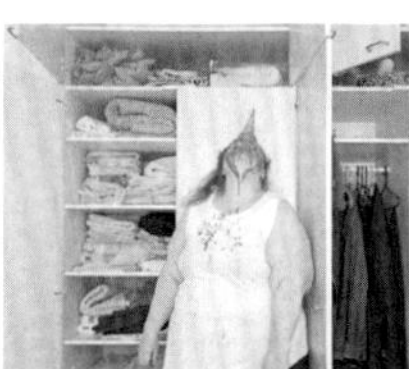

p. 83
*Yksisarvinen - suklaa
(Unicorn - chocolate)*, 2017
Chromogenic print
10 7/16 x 13 11/16" (26.5 x 34.7
cm) (framed)
Collection Martin and
Rebecca Eisenberg

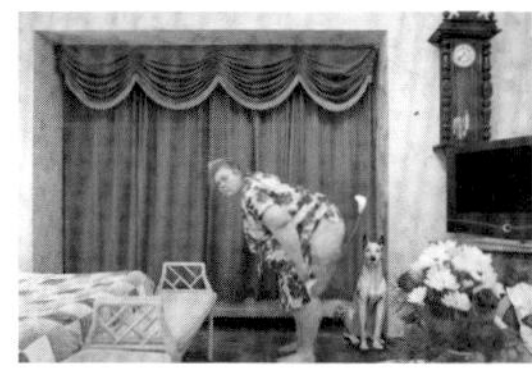

p. 84
Vase, 2017*
Chromogenic print
9 ¼ x 12 ¾" (23.4 x 32.4 cm)

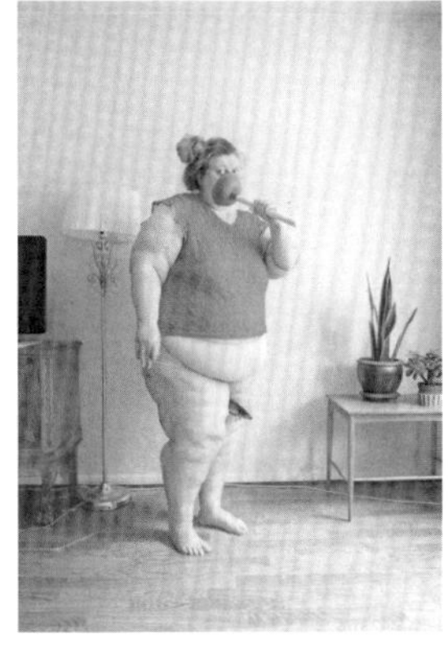

p. 101
A style called a dead fish,
2018
Chromogenic print
24 x 16" (61 x 40.6 cm)
Courtesy the artist and
Makasiini Contemporary

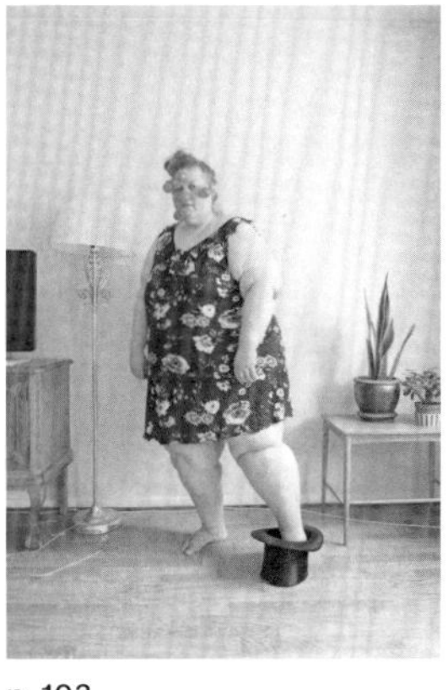

p. 103
*Clown is trying to be
magician's bunny*, 2018
Chromogenic print
24 x 16" (61 x 40.6 cm)
Courtesy the artist and
Makasiini Contemporary

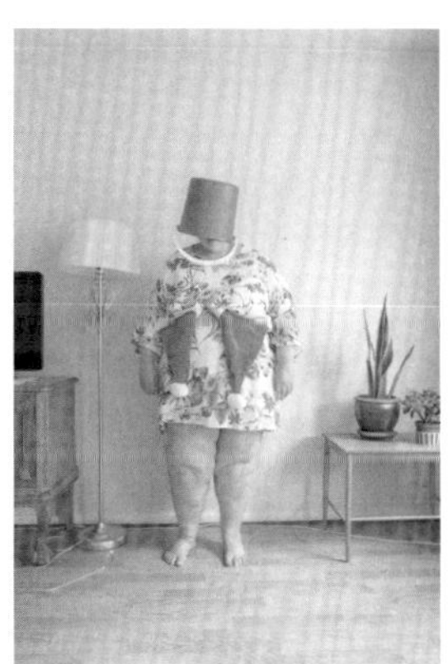

p. 105
Ready for Christmas dinner,
2018*
Chromogenic print
26 x 18" (66 x 46 cm)

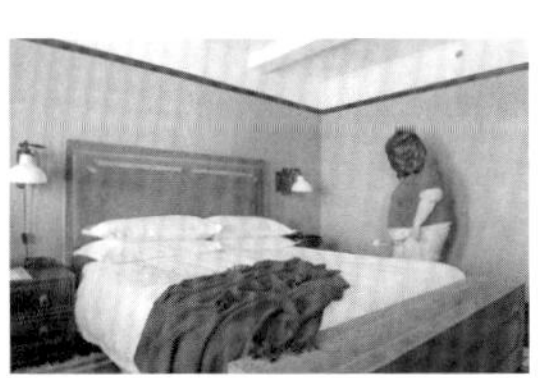

p. 106
Badminton, 2018
Chromogenic print
10 x 15" (25.4 x 38.1 cm)

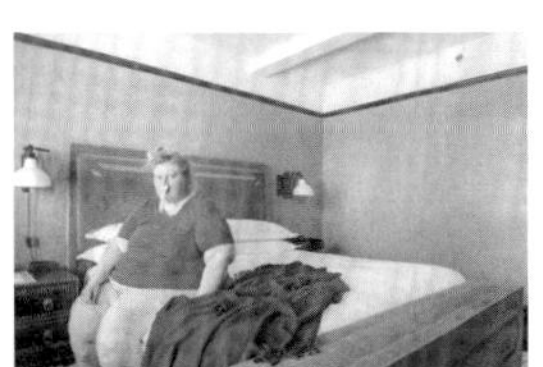

p. 108
Pinocchio, 2018
Chromogenic print
10 x 15" (25.4 x 38.1 cm)

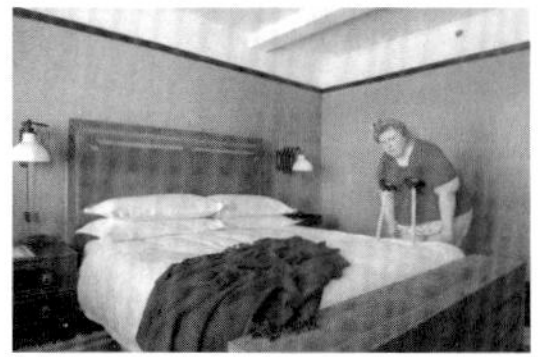

p. 109
Functional, 2018*
Chromogenic print
13 ¾ x 20" (35 x 51 cm)

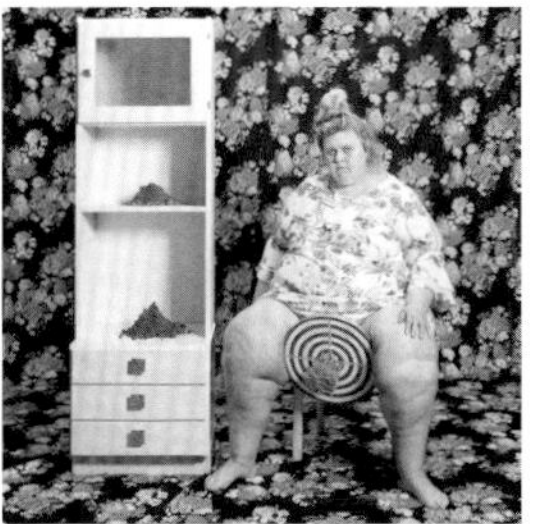

p. 111
Fun, sand and sun, 2018*
Chromogenic print
23 ⅜ x 23 ⅜" (67 x 67 cm)

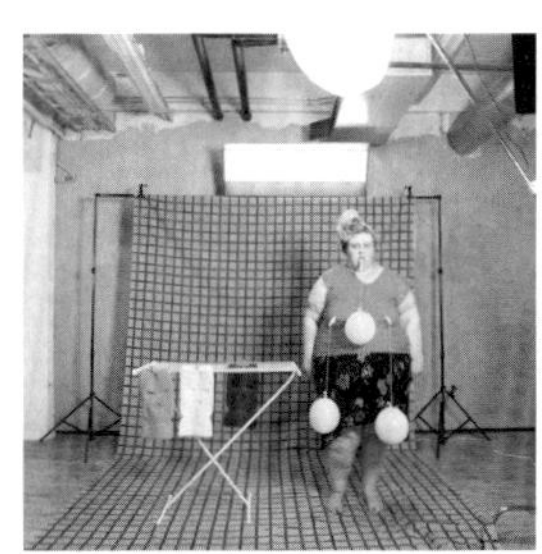

p. 113
Laundry day, 2018*
Chromogenic print
23 ⅜ x 23 ⅜" (67 x 67 cm)

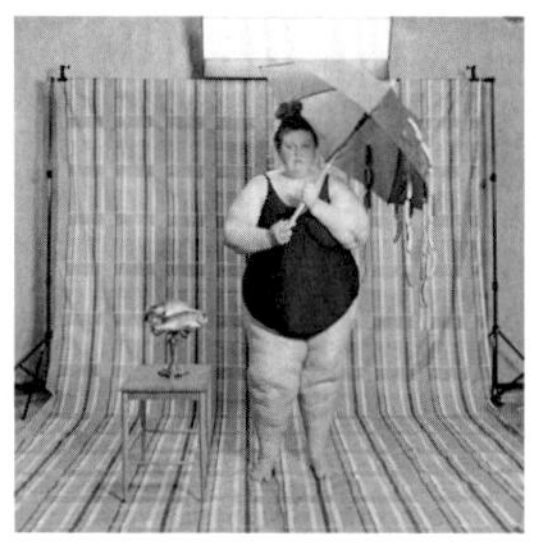

p. 115
Sausage cupid, 2019
Chromogenic print
30 1/2 x 30 1/2" (77.5 x 77.5 cm)
(framed)
Collection Kenny Schachter

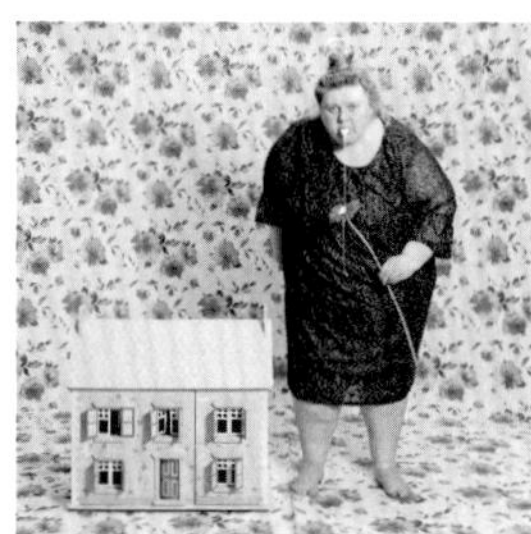

p. 117
Homemade anarchy, 2019
Chromogenic print
23 5/8 x 23 5/8" (60 x 60 cm)
Courtesy the artist and
Makasiini Contemporary

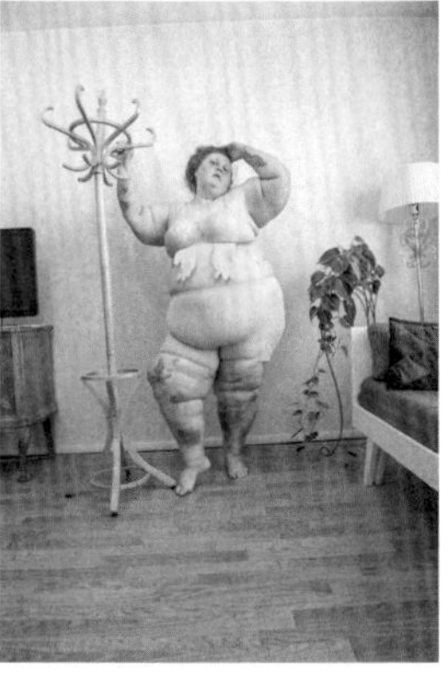

p. 119
Gloves, 2019
Chromogenic print in artist's
frame
21 1/2 x 15 7/8" (54.6 x 40.3 cm)
(framed)
Collection Loren Pack
and Rob Beyer

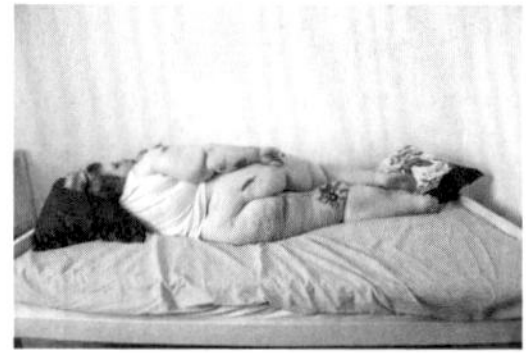

p. 120
Pinwheel, 2019
Chromogenic print in artist's
frame
15 7/8 x 21 1/2" (40.3 x 54.6 cm)
(framed)
Collection Loren Pack
and Rob Beyer

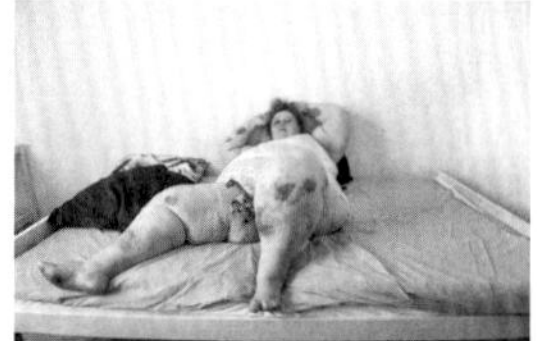

p. 121
Horse, 2019
Chromogenic print in artist's
frame
15 7/8 x 21 1/2" (40.3 x 54.6 cm)
(framed)
Collection Loren Pack
and Rob Beyer

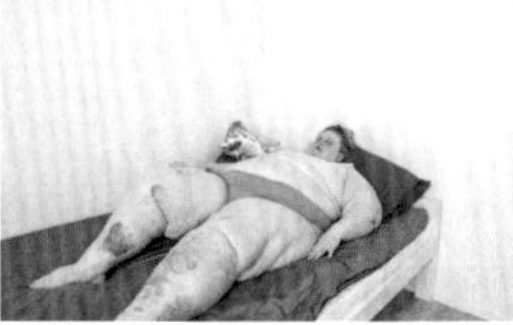

p. 122
Fork, 2019*
Chromogenic print in artist's
frame
15 7/8 x 21 1/2" (40.3 x 54.6 cm)
(framed)

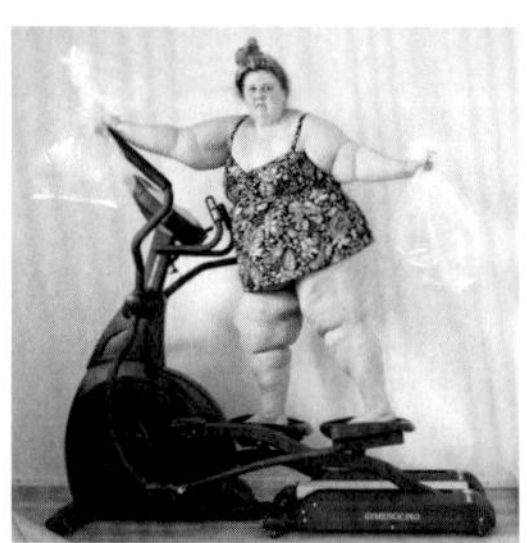

p. 125
Airplane, 2020
Chromogenic print
13 3/4 x 13 3/4" (34.9 x 34.9 cm)
Courtesy the artist and Nino
Mier Gallery

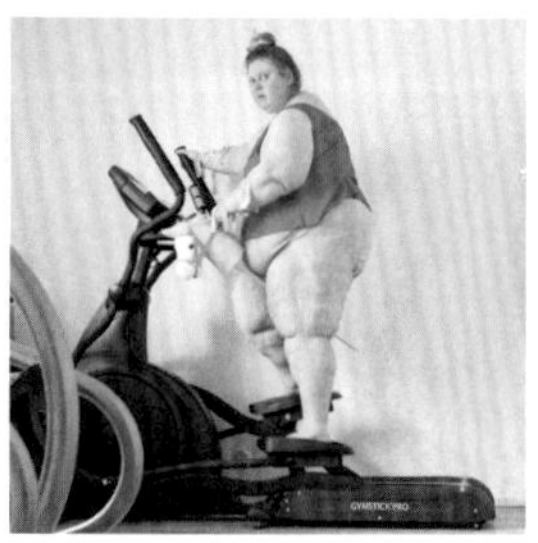

p. 127
Rider, 2020
Chromogenic print
13 3/4 x 13 3/4" (34.9 x 34.9 cm)
Courtesy the artist and Nino
Mier Gallery

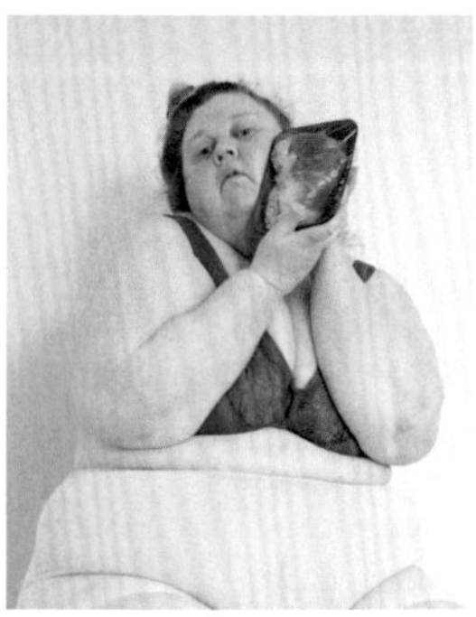

p. 128
Meat Model 1, 2020
Chromogenic print
31 1/2 x 24 3/4" (80 x 62.9 cm)
Courtesy the artist and Nino
Mier Gallery

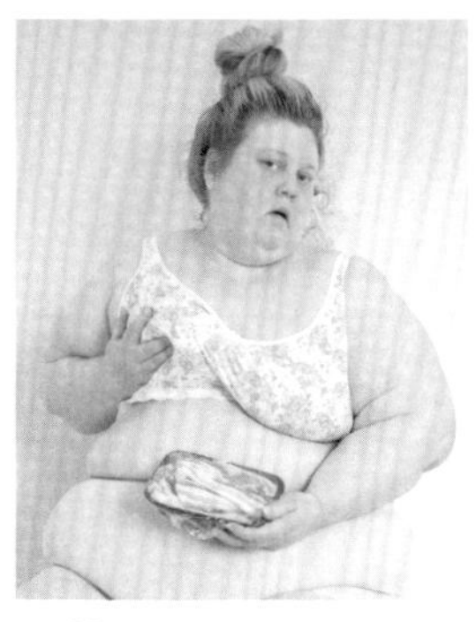

p. 129
Meat Model 2, 2020
Chromogenic print
31 ½ x 24 ¾" (80 x 62.9 cm)
Courtesy the artist and Nino
Mier Gallery

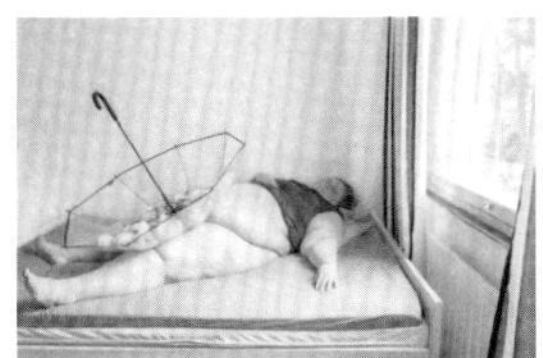

p. 131
Fountain, 2021
Chromogenic print
26 x 38" (66 x 96.5 cm)
Courtesy the artist and Nino
Mier Gallery

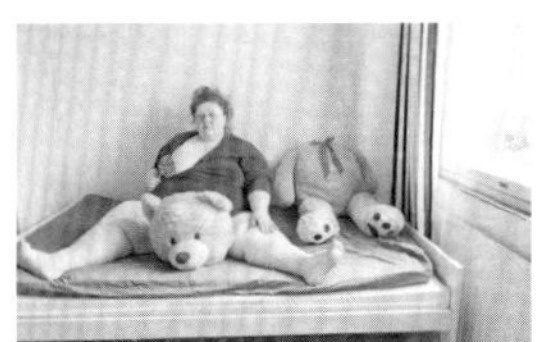

p. 132
Zoo, 2021
Chromogenic print
26 x 38" (66 x 96.5 cm)
Courtesy the artist and Nino
Mier Gallery

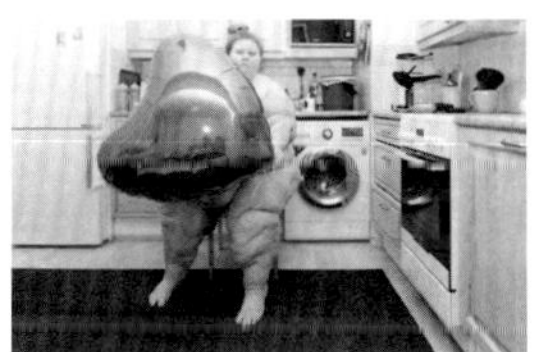

p. 135
Happy Valentines Day (Big Heart), 2022
Chromogenic print
13 x 20" (33 x 50.8 cm)
Courtesy the artist and Nino
Mier Gallery

Videos exhibited:

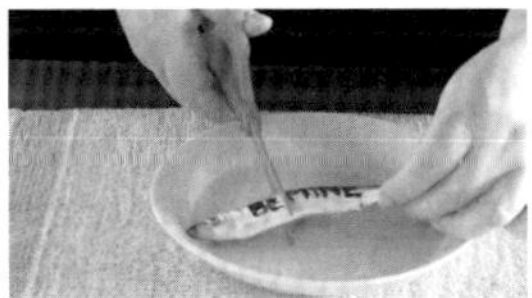

Herring, 2012
Video (color, sound)
1 min, 13 sec

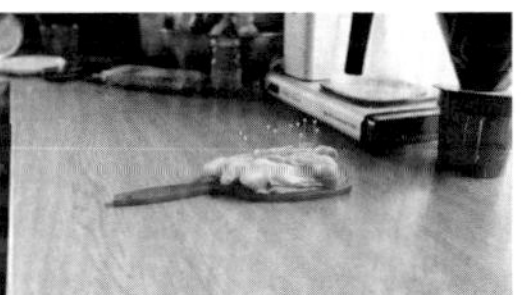

Mirror, 2015
Video (color, sound)
1 min, 47 sec

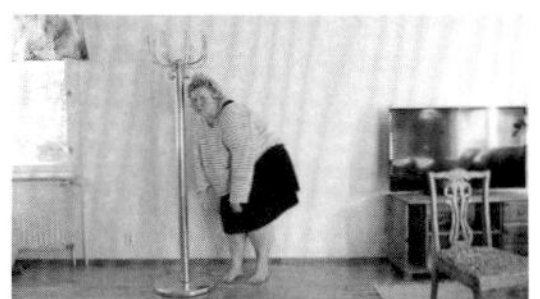

Stand, 2016
Video (color, sound)
51 sec

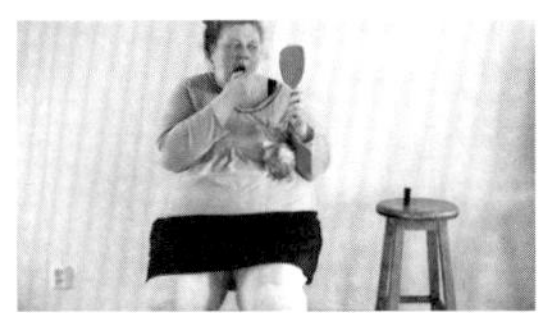

Hearty, 2016
Video (color, sound)
1 min, 21 sec

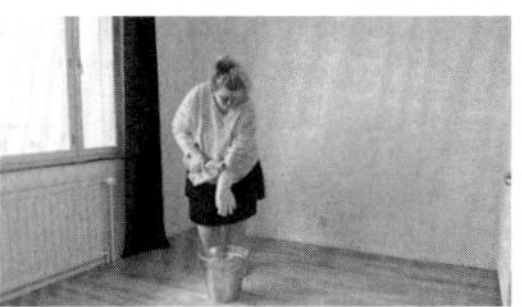

Cow, 2017
Video (color, sound)
1 min, 53 sec

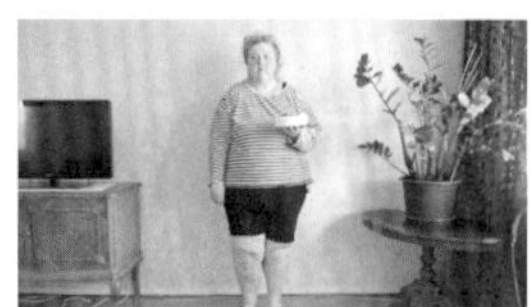

Lunch Box, 2017
Video (color, sound)
34 sec

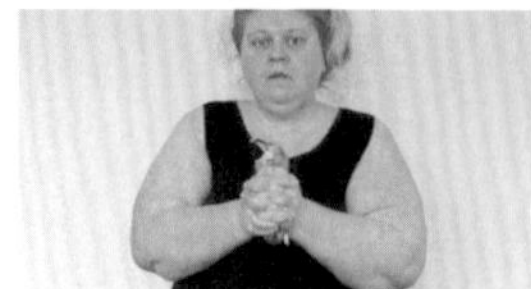

Prayer, 2017
Video (color, sound)
41 sec

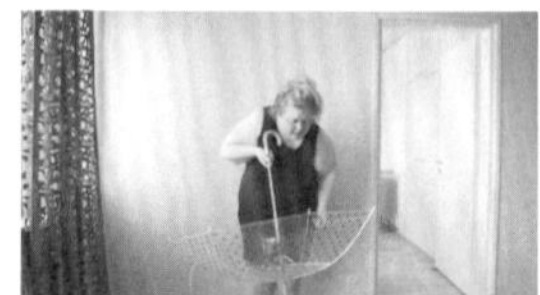

Raining 1, 2017
Video (color, sound)
1 min, 10 sec

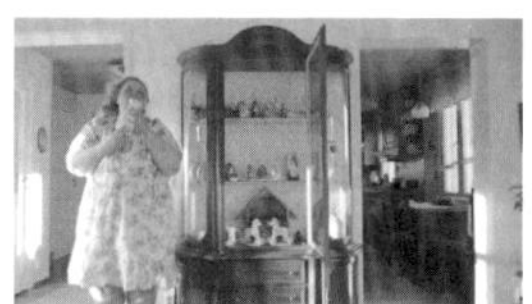

Vitrin, 2017
Video (color, sound)
1 min, 4 sec

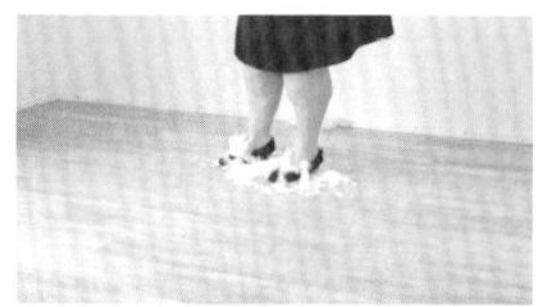

Wanton, 2017
Video (color, sound)
1 min, 7 sec

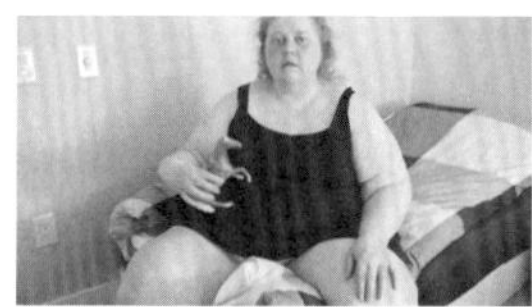

Play with me (Horse), 2018
Video (color, sound)
1 min, 10 sec

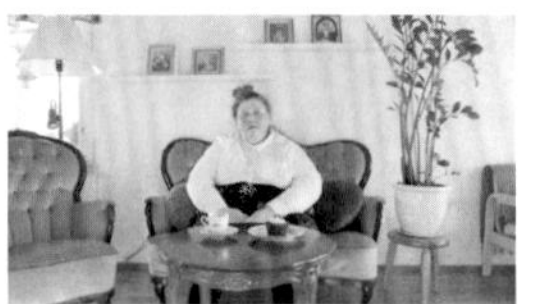

Coffee moment, 2020
Video (color, sound)
1 min, 34 sec

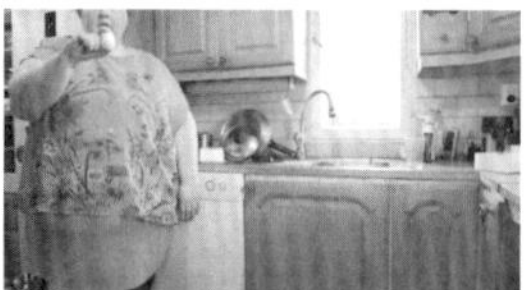

Humble omelet, 2020
Video (color, sound)
39 sec

Unless otherwise noted,
works are courtesy the artist,
Makasiini Contemporary, and
Nino Mier Gallery.

Dimensions reflect print size for
exhibition at MoMA PS1. Works
marked with an asterisk are not
included in the exhibition.

MoMA PS1
Staff List

Andrea Achelis
Visitor Engagement Associate

Marissa Alper
Digital Marketing & Media Fellow

Herbert Armstrong
Maintenance Technician

Arnold Ayala
Maintainer

Philip Brand
Development Associate, Foundation and Corporate Relations

Sham Budhu
Maintenance Technician

Natalie Cheney
Assistant Manager of Visitor Engagement

Stephanie Dias
External Affairs Assistant

Lauren DiLoreto
Director of Program Production

Jonathan Gardenhire
Assistant Director of Individual Giving

Jody Graf
Assistant Curator

Anna Grofik
Preparator

Odean Groves
Maintainer

Lilly Hern-Fondation
Senior Project Manager, Exhibitions and Commissions

Sarah Isenberg
Digital Marketing Coordinator

Shamar Johnson
Administration & Human Resources Fellow

Ruba Katrib
Curator & Director of Curatorial Affairs

Elena Ketelsen González
Assistant Curator

Molly Kurzius
Director of External Affairs

Yasmel Lorenzo
Senior Accountant

Karla Medina
Visitor Engagement Associate

Janggo Mahmud
Public Programs & Community Engagement Fellow

Dante Osei
Director of Finance

Jose Ortiz
Deputy Director

Jose Paz
Maintenance Technician

Dianne Ramoutar
Manager of Human Resources

Jack Radley
Editor

Kari Rittenbach
Assistant Curator

Kate Robinson
Senior Registrar

Kimberly Rodriguez
Staff Accountant

Nora Rodriguez
Digital Strategy & Content Manager

Andrea Sanchez
Administrative Assistant, Curatorial

Julia Schäfer
Graphic Designer

Jinelle Thompson
Manager of Strategic Partnerships

Andley Tyson
Visitor Engagement Associate

Richard Wilson
Exhibition & Production Designer

Laura Zapp
Assistant Director of Visitor Engagement

Published on the occasion of the exhibition *Iiu Susiraja: A style called a dead fish* at MoMA PS1, Long Island City, NY, April 20–September 4, 2023. Organized by Jody Graf, Assistant Curator, MoMA PS1.

Iiu Susiraja: A style called a dead fish is supported by Frame Contemporary Art Finland.

Special thanks to the Consulate General of Finland in New York and the Finnish Cultural Institute in New York.

Support for this publication is provided by Makasiini Contemporary and Nino Mier Gallery.

A CIP record for this book is located at the Library of Congress.

ISBN 9781636811086

Available through D.A.P./Distributed Art Publishers
75 Broad Street, Suite 630
New York, NY 10004
www.artbook.com

Edited by Jody Graf
Designed by Julia Schäfer and Rok Hudobivnik
Copyedited by Dana Kopel

This publication is typeset in Lausanne 400 and printed on Munken Kristall Rough 120 gsm, Arctic Volume High White 115 gsm, and Brossulin XT Tela 210.

Printed and bound in Italy by Grafiche Veneziane

Cover: Iiu Susiraja, *Mad bunny*, 2019 (detail)

Published by MoMA PS1
22-25 Jackson Avenue
Long Island City, NY 11101
www.momaps1.org